The Feminine Principle

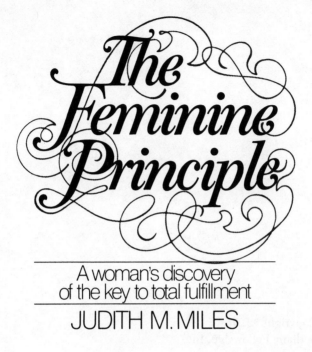

The Feminine Principle

A woman's discovery
of the key to total fulfillment

JUDITH M. MILES

BETHANY FELLOWSHIP, INC.
Minneapolis, Minnesota

Copyright © 1975
Bethany Fellowship, Inc.
Published by Bethany Fellowship, Inc.
6820 Auto Club Road, Minneapolis, Minnesota 55438

Printed in the United States of America

Library of Congress Cataloging in Publication Data:

Miles, Judith M   1937-
    The feminine principle.

    1. Femininity (Psychology)   2. Feminism.
3. Sex role. I. Title.
HQ1206.M46   301.41'2   75-5828
ISBN 0-87123-159-X

DEDICATION

To Keith S. MacLaughlin,
who went on ahead to help with the building

Judith M. Miles

Mrs. Miles describes herself, with characteristic modesty, as a woman who "has astoundingly received grace and mercy from the Lord despite her resurgent pride of intellect and hardness of heart."

But there is much more to her personal story than this self-effacing summary:

She was born in Michigan, lived through her teens and twenties in Colorado, and spent several years in upstate New York.

She is married (happily) and the mother of three teenage children.

Mrs. Miles took her B.A. (cum laude) in English Literature from the University of Colorado, was elected to Phi Beta Kappa, and has a master's degree from the same institution. She has also done doctoral study in English Literature at the University of Denver.

A member of the Lutheran Church–Missouri Synod, she is usually involved in two or three church-related activities at any given time and has been a foster parent to teenagers as a further expression of "the feminine principle."

Contents

Preface

I have come to believe that the only words that communicate something original from God's life to others are words that share what God has worked out in an individual life. We conquer vast schemes of deception by "the blood of the Lamb and the word of our testimony." Just as the Word became a Person in history, so even now we have only those words to share which God has actually wrought into our Christian experience. Other words may be true, may be beautifully put together, may be mentally stimulating, but they are lifeless.

The primary chapters in this book have been worked out by God in my own life. The response letters from Anne, which are fictional, are included as counterpoint; the purpose behind them is to clarify the letters born of experience. However, all in the Anne letters is also authentic in the sense that I have experienced persons who think and act as those represented in the fiction. There is a real Anne, who startled me into writing the book, but she resembles the finished character only in name. I have deliberately given Anne and Peter only parabolic depth so that they might represent any of us.

Judith M. Miles

November 22, 1974

Dear Anne

I cannot remain silent any longer as I watch you struggling in the current surge of feminism. There is a lively alternative. I have some hard-won thoughts about women's liberation and the intrinsic nature of our sex that I will share with you over the next few weeks. Perhaps by writing my experiences to you, I can show you another path, so that when you make your choice you are as wise as a young woman can be about the alternatives. You clearly must make a choice; no longer does the social structure decide for you. That is good, but that also makes you responsible for choosing wisely. Take, then, the admonitions of the "liberators" and weigh them against the thoughts which I will relate to you. Discard nothing merely because it is traditional; many traditions have their roots in reality even though the tradition itself seems deadly. Discard only that which is unreal and illusory.

I identify closely with you in your struggle, because I have struggled too. There are those dear, unruffled ladies who have never had the thought that their personal role in life might need definition and who wonder what all the fuss is about. I marvel at them, but I am not one of them. Every conviction that I now hold has been attacked internally and externally and has been defended.

Anne, you are intelligent, attractive, personable, and open-minded. I take this means of communicating with you so that you may ponder what I have to say in privacy, without the burden of an expected response. I also intend to be very frank about what is psychologically intimate, and I shall be better able to do that with pen and paper.

I am hesitant to mention specific qualifications, since being a thinking woman today ought to be qualification enough for communication on this subject. But I do want you to know that the options among which I choose are real ones. It is sufficient to say that I have had the education and capabilities that would make a very different life—a self-serving one—quite feasible. Instead I have freely chosen a life which on the surface appears to be an ordinary and traditionally Christian one. But I have uncovered a hidden ore in its depths. God has called us to be His friends, and to His friends He reveals in stages the whys of His prescriptions for a fulfilled life. He fashioned Eve most carefully and gave her to Adam, but He left Eve free to discover the intricacies and delights of that relationship with man, or to abuse and distort it. We still have that choice.

I would not write to you if I were still searching and uncertain. I have found deep and abiding joy that is curiously entwined with my womanliness.

Come with me to trace the fine patterns made by the tendrils of joy and the feminine nature. They grow together but have separate roots. Only death can untwine them. That is because womanliness is fashioned into my soul and my body, but joy clothes my spirit.

Our women's movement is a wave on the sea of human unrest, but it appears to be of tidal wave proportions. Many women, like yourself, have been stirred up from complacency into a froth of questioning. In times of personal crisis, we humans are most open to change, to new ways of thinking, to growth. I ask you as a fair-minded seeker of truth to set aside your stereotypes of Christianity, your bad experiences with "Christians," your negative conditioning, and to consider afresh the things that I will share with you. I promise that I will be totally honest with you.

I found my feminine nature, completed and enhanced, when I submitted to the God-man, Jesus Christ. Ultimately all questions of quality or meaning of life, or of the value of persons, are answered in the focal point of history, in Jesus of Nazareth.

Sometimes I am amazed at the demands of zealous Christians that a nonbeliever in their presence ought to give over his very life to Jesus without offering a shred of evidence, other than their evident enthusiasm, that this would be a wise thing to do. It is God's prerogative, of course, to convince instantaneously if He so desires. But most of us need some practical evidence, shown in the lives of other humans, that Christianity really is the truth and that it works. In our complex society made up of thousands of self-contained sub-systems, a man or woman might live his entire life quite isolated from meaningful contact with Christians. That is why I want to share my supply of evidence with you, as God has given it to me.

I shall explore with you first the most simple principle of the true feminine nature—woman as pleasure-giver, primarily to men, but also to other women and to children. I do not mean pleasure in its hedonistic sense; that needs no glorification here. Most of us pass through the world's mirror house of illusions only to discover that no sensuous pleasure satisfies for long. I do not scorn the God-given sensory pleasures, but I am more than the sum of my tingling nerve ends. After I show you the primary principle of woman as pleasure-giver, I will lead you further if you would like to come with me.

Sincerely,
Judith

Dear Judith

I was surprised to hear from you, but I am touched that you took the time to write. It is no burden to respond to you. I much prefer a dialogue situation. You know how I love to get my opinion into a conversation!

I don't feel as though I'm "struggling" with feminism. I think that we are at last speaking up after centuries of silence and repression. I consider myself liberated. Peter understands my point of view and respects it—he even defends the feminist posture in a mixed group. We have come to a comfortable, mutually supportive life-style. I do want to hear what you have to say, though, because part of my philosophy is to value every person's thought when honestly shared.

I cannot accept tradition as a justification for anything. If there is a logic or reason behind any given tradition that is more than a gimmick to preserve the reigning power structure, I'll gladly hear it. If you remember from our wedding, Peter and I kept a small part of the tradition but enriched the service with our individual contributions, like the personal vows we wrote, the wild daisies, and the brown health bread instead of wedding cake.

I'm puzzled that you don't seem to think that I'm a Christian. We don't think that the church-thing makes one a Christian. Most of the values I accept agree with Christianity. We feel especially strong about loving all people. And the sisterhood believes that we should fight for the highest potential of each individual woman—that's certainly Christian! I feel that God loves me, not just a female body with a role expectation to perform until I drop dead!

I'll make no comment on the pleasure-giving until I hear about it, except that I think it's a two-way street between man and woman. I've got to run, as my lunch hour is over.

Sincerely,
Anne

Dear Anne

The feminist is right in declaring that a woman is infinitely more than her biological function and her conforming role in society. I, too, am a feminist, if to be a feminist means to seek the highest potential of each individual woman. The vociferous women who would change our life styles are outraged by the many symptoms of a root disorder. They speak out with righteous (and unrighteous) indignation against the manipulation of women as sex objects, against job and pay discrimination, against unequal opportunities in the educational and political areas, against the unequal bearing of family responsibilities and the dullness of "women's work." They seek recognition of women as primarily people and only secondarily as a gendered subclass. Some of these complaints are just, and redress appears to be coming. But the root problem is the question of human worth, and it is the male problem too. Men who are oppressive and repressive of women are merely diverting attention from their own internal panic. Natural women on top of the power heap are just as cruel and repressive. It is the nature of the human, unregenerated, to repress someone weaker.

What the angry women are really saying is that they feel that their minds and personalities—their personal sets, attitudes, memories, desires, emotions, capabilities—are not being responded to during their sexual contacts nor are they being recognized in their educational, political, or professional pursuits. But the hunger is for more than sex or proficiency or opportunity or recognition. The hunger is undefinable until it is satisfied. When it is satisfied the happy human being can laugh in retrospect and say, "No, it wasn't more sex or more prestige or more recognition that I needed!"

We women are having an identity crisis of huge proportions, but we have been confused into thinking that the whole solution is somehow tied into our gender. By thinking that, *we* are being sexist. We do not have a female problem as much as a human problem. If "they" are male chauvinist pigs, then "we" are chauvinist sows—we're all in the same muddy pen. The solution to human self-ishness and repression is found in Jesus, who alone can change the human situation. Nothing ever really changes without Him. The new life that springs up within the person who is committed to Jesus is a *spiritual* life, but since we are persons with gender, the expression of that life is inevitably shaped by our sex. There are two deep sadnesses that I see in the women's movement: first, the sadness of those who do not know that what women are seeking is found in Jesus; second, the sadness of those who do not know the meaning of femininity and its expression.

There is a crucial aspect of the "sex-object" protest which we must deal with before we can consider woman as pleasure-giver. The dissatisfied women in our age are saying, "You are not touching *me* yet!"—even in relationships between partners who share their minds and emotions and memories freely. Many persons with a "satisfactory sex-life" still feel "sexually" hungry. What then? The natural and usual response is to seek variety, another partner or many, in succession or concurrently. Whether done in imagination or in reality, many people seek a ready quantitative answer to a qualitative problem.

Whenever man or woman is considered as a divided creature who can function on one level (the physical) without involving the other level (mind and personality), one gets into practical and philosophical difficulties. But man considered as a body-mind-personality integrated totality is not sufficient either. For many years I sloshed about in a mental soup that resulted from dividing the human into only two categories, the physical and the non-physical. This is a pervasive intellectual error. The non-physical is for most of us a conglomerate pot of "everything else" called variously "mind," "soul," the "personality," the "true person"—a whole list of leaky categories. Philosophy and psychology have been of little help in straining the pot. But then, with the characteristic shock of truth, the soup was clarified for me. *Three* distinct parts, not two, are involved in any human act—the body, the soul (which is mind, personality, habits, emotions, memories), and *the spirit*. This may never have been vague or confused for you (it's a very old distinction), but for many years I had considered "soul" and "spirit" to be roughly synonymous. They are not. They most decidely are not.

The restlessness of even the sexually active person who is "relating significantly" to someone is the hunger cry of the spirit-person. Now I do not believe that the spirit-person in each of us is either male or female, but his fulfillment is inextricably bound up in the femininity or masculinity of the soul and body. He is ministered to through them, or he is starved to death through them. Until he is filled, the soul and body continue to feel sexual incompleteness, because the soul and body have gender, and incompleteness is translated by them into a sexual metaphor. The liberationists attack this metaphor, sensing correctly that it is not the "real" value of persons, but they do not know what the "real" value is. For some chosen ones, the soul and the body relinquish their sexual activities when the spirit is satisfied because they no longer want the means to an end which is already achieved. These are the true celibates, for whom the metaphor is an embellishment. But most of us need to follow the symbolic route to the same end—the fulfillment of the spirit. We need to begin with the metaphor and to work toward an understanding of the actual. Sexuality, or gender, is ultimately and at its best a symbol which only achieves its fullness when put into the whole poem. But more about that in another letter.

Deep, deep, deep inside, the strident women know that their spirits are not being strengthened as they could be by their relationship to men. If I may translate for them, their words mean, "If you must objectify me, think of me as a cup, for in you is an obstructed source of strength, and that fount of strength could be loosed to refresh both of us—if we only knew how . . . ."

Fondly,
Judith

Dear Judith

I've never thought about having a spirit separate from my personality, but I can relate to the hunger part. Even with Peter I find myself wondering, "Is this all there is to it?", and then I feel guilty because I really do love him. Peter is traveling this week, so I have some extra time to think about us.

Interestingly enough, I never think of Peter or Father or my boss nor any man that I know really well as "the oppressor." It seems to be the whole class of men generally that hold women down. I've met a few that I suspect are thoroughly repressive, however. Your point about women in power (when they get there!) is well taken. I've had a few teachers who had a real put-down for me, but I attributed that to jealousy or frustration in their own thwarted ambition. I think I agree that there is something rotten in all of us—at least in the people I've known. But, then, we've never had the perfect upbringing, the perfect education, the perfect opportunity. Naturally frustration produces anger and other unpleasant things. But as women are freed to contribute their energies and insights fully into the human stream, won't society get far better since our good ideas and constructive thinking have been hampered for so many centuries?

I wish I could believe that the answer was as simple as just Jesus alone. But I'll keep listening. Who knows completely the meaning of femininity? It's a very complex question and each of us knows just parts. Likewise the "real" value of persons.

I've always felt that "Christians" thought that sexuality was at the opposite end of the pike from spirituality. So I'm kind of hooked on your argument that sex is a metaphor for the spiritual actuality. Please elaborate, but remember, I'm no mystic.

In your first letter you said that the true feminine nature is woman as pleasure-giver. I think that I like to pleasure Peter in one way or another because it gives me pleasure to do so. And he responds in kind, of course. Isn't all human motivation basically selfish? And isn't the pleasure of religious people to be able to meet satisfactorily their self-imposed and manageable standards? Really, all human activity can be reduced to the pursuit of pleasure or the avoidance of pain. What more is there to it?

Well, I'd best seek some pleasure in the refrigerator. I never cook when Peter is gone.

Hungrily,
Anne

Dear Anne

The highest good to which a woman may aspire is to give pleasure. This is the feminine principle. But wait—don't turn away in anger until I have qualified my outrageous generalization. Perhaps you may begin to see what has slowly been crystallizing, in a dazzling way, before my eyes. This feminine principle transcends the Orient and the Occident, which we assume to be irreconcilable in terms of womanship. This feminine principle transcends the range of delicate toddler through wrinkled great-grandmother. But it is especially vital to those of us within the long season of our sexual bloom.

I must begin with the obvious, an assumption from design. As the bird's wing is exquisitely fashioned to allow it to fly, so also a woman is beautifully made to give pleasure. Consider how our voices are modulated for melody rather than volume; a loud woman is experienced unpleasantly in any circumstance, but a loud-speaking male is often experienced as appropriate. Melody is for pleasure; volume, for necessity. Consider how our shape elicits a distinctive response of pleasure in our men, while men's bodies are mostly experienced as beautiful only after they are invested (by the viewer) with symbolic value; that is, I find a man attractive in shape because he is intelligent, loyal, kind, brave, generous, witty, godlike, and so on. Consider how our innately gentler disposition is ideally suited for the comfort of wounded and weary creatures, from babies to ill people or pets, but especially for world-sick husbands and children. We appear to be fashioned for pleasure-giving by our Creator.

But an even more telling reason to keep ourselves primarily pleasure-givers will become immediately obvious if we imagine a strictly utilitarian world. In some primitive societies or poverty areas where both sexes must unite in a grim struggle for mere survival, there is little time for laughter or beauty or joy. But wherever the men are capable of providing adequately the inevitable specialization is found: man works and fights; woman, delights. In this century materialistic societies have sought to divert their woman power into utilitarian roles and have succeeded in an astonishing measure. Most of these working women have not-too-demanding jobs that permit them to carry on their pleasure-giving activities on a diminished scale. The little touches that make life for others an excursion rather than a dreary trudging—a game with the children, homemade cinnamon buns, a bikeride together at evening, a visit with a lonely old person—must be forgotten by the ambitious woman.

It is sad that all of us creatures of delight fail in some measure to distribute the packets of light and joy entrusted to us for delivery. (Don't smirk yet, please.) How many strangers are left bereft of the

24

quick smile that could have been theirs! How we starve even our loved ones! Lest you think I am turning sickly sentimental, or already have, I hasten to tell you that I knew that we were for pleasure-giving intuitively for a long while (as most of us do) before I saw *why* it must be so. I have come to believe that God has entrusted to our feminine keeping much of that which will make human spirits ravenous for Himself, here on earth and ultimately in heaven. We are the very imperfect vessels that He has chosen to carry solid hints of His merciful nature to the world of men and babies. To the males, made in God's image, is entrusted the communication of the godly attributes of power and law—and judgment. And who of us seeks avidly to be subject to power or judged by law? Only after God is experienced as love do we delight in His majesty. Before that we are just plain scared of Him. When we hear words like "God is love," the content is meaningless until we have experienced human love, and human love is primarily transmitted by mothers, or men and women together who have been loved by their mothers. What we know of peace, of order, of cleanness, of purity, of beauty, of joy, of gentleness, of fidelity, of virtue, we know primarily from women, and only secondarily from men who have learned from their mothers. Everybody really knows this. The old double standard of morality, the respect and sheltering accorded the woman (until she shows herself to be unworthy), is deeper than cultural; it is recognition of innate qualities. Folk wisdom knows this, "A man's character rarely rises above that of his wife, and certainly not above that of his mother." Why God has entrusted the most precious jewels in the universe—mercy, love, and tenderness—to our keeping I do not know, but He has.

But what happens when we fill our hours with competing and acquiring? The reminders of God's loving nature to the dusty and bewildered world lie hidden, or worse yet, are spilled out and lost. Little ones grow up barren. Dry-throated and weary husbands forget the taste of joy or remember it only as something lost in youth along with innocence. And so the dissolute world begins to forget to seek for God, because man's appetite for Him is atrophied. When we of the pleasure realm wander into the power realm, we leave our ability to image part of God behind us, and in the power realm we are nothing but naked phonies. Bad enough, but worse still, we partially emasculate our husbands by doing so and hopelessly distort our sons and daughters who have a satisfactory model for neither love nor law. If the world no longer knows what love is nor where to find it, how ever can men know God and joy?

In my following letters, I will share with you my discoveries of the woman-life, the feminine pleasure principle.

As always,
Judith

Dear Judith

I'm sorry I've taken so long to answer. I'm stunned by your equations of feminine equals reflected love from God and masculine equals reflected power. In my observations, all of us have some of both qualities. A mother enforces family discipline for the children, and a father can be tender and loving. Perhaps any individual can be located somewhere on a graph with love as feminine one axis and power as masculine the other, just as each individual biologically has a mixture of male and female hormones. Maybe the two are correlated!

But if, as you say, masculine and feminine are different in kind, not in gradation or mixture, there is a point where infinite love and infinite power meet, and that point would be in God. Mother had a favorite saying, "Perfect love casts out fear." That would be true if perfect love and perfect power were the same.

I am not sure that I would know how to please in a way that would reflect God's love, even if I wanted to. I just shared my idea of perfect power and perfect love meeting in one point with Peter, and he said, "Mm-hmm." On a scale of loving from one to ten, I think I'm about a two!

In friendship,
Anne

Dear Anne

Don't worry about being a two. The great thing about performance scales is that God doesn't use them. People do. God looks at the forgiven sinner through the focal point where love and power meet and sees him as perfected because of Jesus, the Reconciler.

In the broad sense of pleasure-giving of which we have spoken, the potential for the creative woman is infinite, since human spirits are eternal. Those whom we love will carry the effects of that love wrought into their spirits forever. And those whom we fail to love may hunger forever, because they may never see past our lovelessness to a God who is love. The seriousness of this realization has been enough to slay personal power-ambition dead in its tracks again and again for me, but ambition has a remarkable resuscitative power. The greatest shock of remorse ever to come to me was at the premature death of a friend. I had given her a scanty measure of love—bits of time from my busy schedule, cheery encouragement, shallow optimism, words about a glorious faith that was, however, bearing only a few dwarfed fruits in my own life. I never reached her need. God has forgiven me, but, Anne, may you never have the hard knowledge that your love was deficient when it really counted.

Let no one deceive you; the currency of the universe is love, and without it, you are bereft of all.

But I want to get down to the practical: how do we, the delights of the earth, go about giving pleasure (if that is our *raison d'etre*) and reflecting the eternal love of God? I will begin with the basic and follow the approximate pattern of my own foliation. The first way of pleasure-giving is through physical beauty.

Though each of us has some external beauties, and God has graciously put a secret desire into the hearts of certain men for large noses, broad hips, or crooked teeth because of a boyhood beloved with those attributes (usually his mother), we are obviously not created equal in the beauty department. Cleanliness, careful clothes selection, exercise, nutritious diet, and enough rest will make any of us pleasant to look upon, but will not make each of us beautiful. Beauty, of course, is a gift of the Creator, like intelligence or grace, scattered without regard to merit of the receiver. We think of beauty as a gift to the beautiful person, and this is our mistake. Beauty is a gift to the race of men, localized in certain individuals, but the delight is for the beholders, the others. The beautiful person, because of evil, is especially subject to the corrosion of vanity and to exploitation by others, or worse yet, to dependence on fading charms.

What is this gift, then, to the beholders? It has two parts, recognition and longing. The recognition is pleasant to both men and women (and children), and a lovely woman will immediately draw the eyes of the crowd. An involuntary sigh or song of praise to the Creator of perfection will rise up, though it may emerge as a wolf whistle or as gutter language. This, by the way, is why natural beauty is always preferred to artificial enhancements. Most often our stultified consciousnesses recognize the beauty without a thought of the source, but we do approve His handiwork. A split second after the recognition comes the longing. Because of our lowly nature the longing is translated by our flesh into either sexual desire or jealousy. Either alternative leads to frustration and anger, except to the mate of the beauty—but that later.

I know that everything that is created is good, because the Creator is good and love. Therefore, not only is beauty good, but the recognition and longing are good too. But because we are warped, we transform the recognition and longing into unlawful desire or jealousy. Consider instead what the recognition and longing aroused by beauty have been created for. I believe that they are perceptions of the spiritual world, cradled in a metaphor that we can feel and understand. Our eternal spirits were made to fit beautiful spiritual bodies that we cannot perceive by any means other than by simile. Those glorious spiritual bodies must somehow be mirrored in the earthly bodies of those we think of as very beautiful. Our buried spirit recognizes the similarity immediately and responds to the picture of its desire and ultimate home. Then comes the ineffable longing—the longing to be free of sin and beautiful and spiritually alert, the dissatisfaction with what we are, the craving for an eternal renewal.

Consider the beauty of the angels (who are sexless) in Christian art. Possibly human beauty awakens an archetype of the angel to our watching spirit. The vernacular is certainly indicative of this possibility, i.e., "you're an angel," "she looked like an angel," etc. Artists know that the young, lovely woman with flowing white robes arouses an inexplicable yearning in each of us. So do the commercial advertisers know this. To dismiss this deep and pervasive yearning as sexual desire is intellectual poverty. And, because of what God is, where there is a yearning, there is a fulfillment. He is not interested in frustrating us; that is the province of evil. He has put the beautiful ones among us to awaken in us the longing for the beauty *we can* have in the new, spiritual order when it comes. But we must rouse ourselves now and begin to seek it. When I hear of someone, "Who does she think she is, God's gift to humanity?" I laugh and praise God for His lavish hints of what is to be for those who love Him.

The very beautiful among us have the superb privilege of being a symbol in God's poem to the human race, unconsciously. What cause for rejoicing among us mortals when those lovely symbols begin to pulse with spiritual life and to transmit willingly

31

some of His glorious attributes, like love and forgiveness, selflessness and humility, true joy and pure laughter.

Next time I'll write about the beauty of the rest of us, Anne, who are a little less than physical perfection.

Until then, reflect!
Judith

Dear Judith

I have always wished that I were beautiful. But my motive in wishing that would be to attract people to myself, not to remind anyone of a spiritual order. I also want Peter to love me more, and I've felt that if only I were more beautiful to him he would. I do feel jealousy when Peter looks at a beautiful girl. Basically, I have a fear that someone more attractive than I am will take his affections away from me. I see that happening often in couples I know. Peter gives no evidence of the slightest interest in anyone else, but the fear is there anyway. I am afraid that I will begin to act jealously and suspiciously and then actually drive him away. I haven't told anyone this before, because I don't like it in myself.

How does a woman handle her beauty problem anyway? Sorry this is so short. I've been waiting for an interview.

Sincerely,
Anne

Dear Anne

I promised to write next about that share of physical beauty entrusted to each of us. You have, as you have discovered, a nice portion of attractiveness. It is every woman's dowry, and if it is not to give pleasure, then, why do we have beauty? To please ourselves? I think not, since vanity is universally unloved. To please the world? Yes, in the general, symbolic way I spoke of in my last letter. But the secret purpose enlivening beauty is specifically to please one man. Since man has an infinite potential for individuality, only an infinite variety of beauties supplies one for each special desirer. The coltish teen years and early twenties are fraught with the energy-consuming selection process for most of us. In the sub-group elected by each person to his "acceptable" category, the operation of other selection variables comes into play (hopefully). A few rare perceptive individuals, especially girls, or some more mature mate-seekers agewise, are not influenced by physical beauty at all. As the facts stand, however, in our culture most of us choose first mates at a rather primitive level, emotionally rather than rationally or spiritually, and physical beauty *is* a major selection factor. But remember, each of us has a capacity for an individual ideal of beauty based more on past experience than on the media image.

I am interested in showing what happens after selection and commitment to one mate. We can assume in most young couples an initial bond of mutual physical attraction. That is a real plus, a one-up on the divorce statistics to start with, but what happens next? If we asked a number of thoughtful persons to give the one overruling characteristic of physical beauty, most would say its fleetingness. Its very transcience is the quality that incites many to an attempted greedy appropriation or a bitter covetousness. Urgency is a major motif in the poets who celebrate physical beauty. This is more of the "object" mentality and a basis for the feminine protest. But beauty is not an object; it is the symbol of a potential reality, a potential restoration. More exactly, it is the outer mold for an inward creative process. Perhaps an analogy will help to explain what physical beauty seems to me.

I visited a rather surprising exhibit of true-to-life busts of American patriots done in bronze. The heads were not sculptures but poured metal molded in casts taken by the artist from his models when they were alive and well in the flesh. Of course now both the models and the artist have long since turned to dust, but the bronze faces are firm and as perpetual as anything terrestrial can be. The bronzing process is a picture of life to me. Look for a moment at the cool serenity of Patriotess A. She, the real personhood of her, the essence, was for a fleeting few moments incorporated into a plaster mass, a suffocating, wet heaviness that cleaved to her and was impressed with her character. Her life was imparted to an earthen cask. Let the life of this cast bearing her imprint represent her life span on this sphere. The mold took on a semblance of delicate beauty for a while, but it was fragile and empty. The artist purposed to fill it with molten metal to create his permanent vision of her beauty. But suppose an interloper, a rival to the artist, sneaks into his workroom and steals the fragile mold before the filling of the hollow within has begun. Perhaps he has a gallery of molds, lined with mirrors, for its display. But after men and children handle it, and the elements gust at it when the doors are opened, and the ordinary wear and tear, heat and cold and dirt of life in the gallery work at it, the beautiful mold begins to crack and crumble, because it was soft and pervious to begin with. The interloper, concerned solely with facades, will discard it, and the wasted mold has no resource within the hollow space nor any beauty left that men should desire her. Her fleeting beauty has betrayed her to herself, and denied the artist's intended perfection.

However, if the interloper is apprehended before he can steal, and the artist's work proceeds as he planned, the fragile mold begins to take into herself the stuff of permanence. The metal is still fluid as it comes—it can slosh out again; the mold might crack and spring a leak, but the metal as it comes from the artist's dipper is a pure, refined experience concocted to create a solid and beautiful good. The molten fluid begins to firm within the mold and gradually acquires a shape. Near the end of the process, the interior person, still unseen, is nearly solid, permanent, and beautiful, while the exterior mold is shopworn and weakened.

Suppose a witness has watched the whole artistic process with a personal involvement—maybe he is the watchman over the mold and a lover of the arts. Would he not at this point "see" the inner bronze person with eyes of deepened love and desire even though the almost discarded mold still covered her? And if he had faithfully suffered with her the fulfillment with the hot metal, and longed through the cooling with her, and was nearly ready to view the glory of the artist's workmanship—would he not have to be deranged to leave her side and take up his watch over a new, still-hollow plaster mold? Has not the tenderness and protectiveness he originally felt toward the earthen mold been gradually transferred to the creation within, to the coming beauty that he has watched through its pain and enlargement until he feels that it is truly his joy and possession?

Anne, the weary world is still full of pathetically eager watchmen-lovers whose strength and virility are being dissipated because beauty refuses to submit to her filling.

Thoughtfully,
Judith

Dear Judith

I'm empty. How do I get filled?

Love,
Anne

Dear Anne

The secret that transports an empty young woman from a limbo of frustrated power-seeking to a garden of pleasure-giving is obedience. It is so simple (as are all truths), yet so utterly inimical to our self-images, so opposite to most of our modern models, so devastating to our pride. Pride. One of the great mysteries of education to me is that we urge all our young and unfortunates to develop pride. Yet we hate pride when we view it in any contemporary or superior. Let me assure you that building pride in self or others is constructing a prison.

The man or woman who attempts to justify God's ways is a fool; we can only observe them in wonder and praise. I have observed this: the way of love, the highest good, is through obedience. The way of Jesus, ultimate Love, was obedience. The way of woman as purveyor of love, divine and human, is obedience. This means obedience to her husband as well as to God. We cannot always see God; our husbands we can see.

The plan is this. Man is created in the image of God, but man (generic) is male and female. We know that we are now, in the natural, imperfect, but the perfect plan remains in effect. The male is invested with attributes of power and justice, like

authority

Tenderness

God's. The female has attributes of mercy and love, like God's. The male is like Law; the female like Gospel, yet they become one flesh, as God is One. If we take just one archetypal couple and their internal relationship, what occurs anew in each marriage, we see the attributes in action. Over whom is the husband to have power and authority, if not the wife? For whom is the wife's overflow of love and tenderness, if not the husband? Each function or working out of the innate attributes is dependent on the other half and his or her response. Now love begets love which in turn begets more love and the two are entwined in a forever-circle of love. Praise God for that! But power is only manifested with a complement of submission. A king with no people is no king. Authority without obedience is impotent. But when the wife in love submits to her husband's authority, he is enthroned and begins to exercise the divine attributes of power— to his own strengthening and to the delight of his wife's secret heart. This awakening of his power potential extends far beyond their home. Thus a woman is not *behind*, but rather is *upholding*, every successful man.

Often the contemporary man is unaware of his real power, since power lines may have been confused in his parental home. If he selects an unsubmissive wife (like mother), he may remain a lifetime in an embryonic state of manhood. A woman who is not under her husband's authority will be discontented. She often seeks authority from other sources—physicians, scholars, clergymen, or occultists. The unsubmitted woman may try herself to fill a dominant, power role, and she is frustrated if she succeeds and frustrated if she fails.

Often, perhaps always, it is the unsubmissiveness of the wife that breaks into the beautiful love circle of the newly married, and breakdown begins. Even the sexual pattern teaches us that the female is to love and submit, the male to love and be submitted to. If our archetypal Eve defies her husband's request or wish or command at some point, he is attacked subtly in his power consciousness, and this inevitably affects his ability to respond with love to her love. At the same time, her love for him is adulterated by her self-serving and by her diminished view of him as a strong male, and the love begets love begets love cycle is weakened. The beautiful plan of a godly, powerful man and a submissive, delightful wife loving and supporting one another in continual refreshment can become instead a farce with a two-headed monster destroying itself in a power struggle.

What does the woman lose by submitting to her own husband? Well, she may lose some pride, a characteristic that makes her universally unlovely to men, women, and God. And she may lose some temporary gratification, that which causes a conflict of wills with her husband—say, a new purchase, a choice of entertainment, even a pattern of living. Especially at first, when living with a man still but roughly shaped by the Lord's hand, she may find submitting to his will in some instances to be very painful. For instance, he may have a differing will on such crucial issues as number of children, duty to parents, and geographical location. But remember love. The submissive and loving wife stirs up all the reservoirs of love and protectiveness in her husband, and an initially harsh husband is becoming a strong and loving one; he need no longer be on the defensive.

The submissive and cheerfully obedient wife may also lose stature in the eyes of her more demanding sisters, but her joy and contentment will puzzle them. How well I remember my wonderment at the gentle attitude of a wife who refused to complain to her husband about his after-work talk sessions that sometimes extended late into the night. I was hurt and angry whenever my young husband joined him without phoning, and I did not hesitate to let my husband know about my anger. Who was the wiser? She was giving to her husband a feeling of manly freedom without a report call home to "mama," a time for recreation with his male friends without feeling guilty. His behavior was undeniably inconsiderate, yet she was greater than his transgression. A put-upon, neglected wife? Hardly. My self-righteous indignation succeeded in spoiling my husband's spontaneous pleasure in these bull sessions, built up in him some resentment against me, chipped away at his vulnerable ego, and caused dissension between us. And he continued in this behavior pattern despite my protests. She built her husband up by silent submission; I tore mine down by complaints and tears.

What does the woman gain by submission to her own husband? Only the infinite security of yielding to the duly constituted chain of authority in the universe; only the deep joy of living with a real man who grows stronger every day; only the fulfillment of fully participating in a genuine love relationship; only the completing of what is partial in her human nature; only the opening of her yielded being to the influence of God's Spirit, who comes where humble and yielded spirits are seeking Him.

Still in wonderment at His ways,
Judith

Dear Judith

Mother sends regards. I'm writing at the glass patio table in the sunshine. The flowers are beautiful here this year. We're visiting Mother for the long weekend. She is well. Peter is preparing a paper and is locked into it mentally, but he emerges now and then for some conversation or refreshment. I haven't discussed your last two letters with him, as they are too heavy for our relationship right now.

I guess I am proud. Obedience sticks in my craw, bluntly. But your reasons keep going through my head. Is it really I who can help Peter to be a strong man like Father, was? I don't mean he's weak. He just avoids decisions and commitments at home.

I find myself deciding what we're going to do on the weekends, or at least suggesting plans that he usually goes along with. If I ask about having someone for dinner, he just says, "I don't care. Do what you'd like." I've never thought of us as having a power struggle. We don't fight much at all.

I think I agree with what you are saying in an ideal sense. But I don't see how it could possibly work for Peter and me. For one thing, he never tells me to do anything directly, so how could I submit to him? For another, there are some areas that I am more competent in than he is—I think my judgment in these areas is better than his. Wouldn't we be losing out as a family if my areas of competency weren't being used in the decision-making process?

Peter doesn't go out for bull sessions without calling. He just stays at the office forever.

I guess I've decided to look for ways to try submission. But if he never shows an authoritative behavior, I'll have an easy out!

> *Tentatively,*
> *Anne*

Dear Anne

All right. I promised to love, honor, and obey him, but it was not that easy. Loving him came naturally;

my beginning love gushed up and overflowed and was supernaturally sustained. Thank God. Honoring I did not know anything about. Obeying was something I gave good lip service to. In practice, I obeyed him when it suited me to do so, and since we were basically compatible, our life was fairly smooth. Love goes a long, long way. But I remember some ugly, wounding scenes, and I see myself in retrospect performing in a most unsubmissive manner. How great is the grace of God to preserve our love despite ourselves!

I was perplexed and bewildered that two who truly loved could experience difficulties in their married state. In my frustration I searched the Scriptures. One day this familiar verse acquired a heightened meaning for me, "Wives, be subject to your husbands, as to the Lord" (Eph. 5:22). It could not mean *that*! Not as to *the Lord*! But there it was. I was to treat my own human husband as though *he* were the Lord, resident in our own humble home. This was truly revelatory to me. Would I ask Jesus a basically maternal question such as, "How are things at the office?" Would I suggest to Jesus that He finish some task around the house? Would I remind the Lord that He was not driving prudently? But it is even more subtle than that. Would I ever be in judgment over my Lord, over His taste, His opinions, or His actions? I was stunned— stunned into a new kind of submission.

Anne, you might think that my personality with him became withered, spineless, or unreal. No. I began

44

to learn to relate to him in his potential dimension, to really love him on a deeper level. I was freed from an imposed mother-reformer-teacher-seducer role that had subtly been present from time to time. As I stripped these roles, I began to discover the "I" that he loved. I was freed to respond fully to him in love and to accept him. I found a new security in our relationship. I watched in astonishment and with thankfulness as he grew stronger and more exciting when he discovered his power hook-up with God. He was created to image forth the glory and power of God. When he no longer had to wrestle with a competitor in his bosom, he was freed to look outwards and upwards. He was being changed by God's Spirit into the likeness of Christ, and I was no longer a hindrance, but a help to him. I am sure the Lord would have accomplished His good work in him without my cooperation and humbling, but who wants to be a thorn in the Lord's work when she might be an enhancement?

But another amazing thing happened. As I willingly yielded to my husband, obeying him in obedience to the Lord's express command, my heart softened towards God himself. I was becoming pliable clay in His hands. The two obediences were inextricably bound up together. Why do you think that often we women seem more naturally to seek God than men do? Are we less sinful? We *know* that is not true. No, the servitude that we render to husbands, to children, to the helpless; the necessary mean tasks that must be done; and most of all, the submission to a husband's authority have the very salutary effect of humbling us. And herein is a beautiful blessing, for God dwells "in the high and holy place, and with [her] of a humble and contrite spirit." When I humbled pride with my husband, praise God, pride sustained a mortal wound. This is part of God's perfect plan for families. If, indeed, the prerequisite to the fullness of God's presence is a humble heart, we women have a blessed head start by the nature of our education and employments. The Lord must use more strenuous means to break the pride of our men folk, and He does break them too, in love. The very nature of the enemy is pride and rebellion. Both are quenched by simple obedience. How easy it is to be a wife! My energies can now be employed in a myriad of joy-filled pursuits. Because marriage is a lifetime contract, I can count on the Lord using my lord during our lifetime together as an effective pride-slayer whenever pride rises again for another round within me (it does). Even more important than in the natural realm, he is a spiritual protector for me when I obey him. I will explain this later.

Now about the "honoring." I think I understand some of this now, though our understanding of truth is always partial, simply because He who is truth is infinite. I thought that the church fathers, or whoever wrote the marriage ceremony, were wrong in their order. *Honor* comes after *obey*, thought I, because when I, as wife, obey consistently, he, as husband, becomes more powerful, more into the image of Christ, more honor-worthy. I was wrong. *Worthiness is never an issue in God's order,* happily for all of us. God alone is worthy. Like mercy, forgiveness, love, and all of God's blessings, honor comes to the husband from the wife (and *vice versa*) simply because God says so. By fiat. You see, Anne, a man in the world has to earn honor—by his hard work, his integrity, his associations, or, more crudely, his money. But no one earns anything in "real life," the kingdom that God is establishing on this earth, coexistent with the world's life but invisible to most. All the gifts to us in God's kingdom are free, by grace. If a wife gives honor freely, from the beginning, to her husband, she is ministering directly one of God's gifts to him. No strings attached. And she is there to give him honor every morning, to build him up for the day; every evening, to neutralize the world's daily dose of poison; every leisure moment shared, to release his reservoirs of good humor; every time of stress, to bolster him. So what if he does not deserve it; none of us deserved God's love either. By giving that poor fellow human being honor (praise God that we have something to give him!), God honors us by allowing us to be His ministers. Love is given that way to one's husband too, of course, unreservedly, and often undeservedly. But you knew that. Even psychotherapists know that. They have to simulate some "unconditional positive regard" to try to undo all the damage done by women too busy to love and honor.

Wistfully,
Judith

Dear Judith

Sorry it's been so long since I've written. I've been trying submission to Peter and it's working. Sometimes. At first I had to search for ways to convey my new attitude toward him without coming right out and saying it. It was a game for a while. For instance, I began consistently to buy his favorite brand of ice cream instead of mine. I didn't ask him to take out the garbage anymore. I didn't initiate any social occasions until he said, "Why don't you ask Bill and Penny over for pizza tomorrow?" I picked up his dirty socks without muttering. I didn't say anything snide about his mother when she came over. I bit my tongue when he put on a blue shirt with a green tie. (It wasn't too bad, after all.) You get the picture. He didn't seem to notice a thing! But he seemed to be getting perceptibly warmer toward me emotionally, though we never have been cold to one another. Then one night (late) he said, "Why don't you take the blue car by the garage tomorrow and have Cindy pick you up for work?" I blew it there.

"Because," I answered sarcastically, "it's ten miles out of her way, and you could do it just as easily and catch the bus."

"Okay," he said. After awhile I knew I'd taken a

giant step backwards. So I started all over again. The next time he suggested something, I remembered and agreed cheerfully, although it was a nuisance to me. I guess it is a pretty humbling process—the ups and downs of it especially. He is becoming more confident in his leadership role. But I'm feeling manipulative, especially when I'm obeying or submitting to his tastes out of principle but my emotions are raging inside. I feel that this behavior is mechanical, that I'm doing the right thing for the wrong reason. I feel like a hypocrite. I don't feel that God is with me and that I'm doing His thing in obeying Peter. How do I know?

Vacillating,
Anne

Dear Anne

I do not really know anything about the depth of your commitment to God; that is between Him and you, of course. The feminine principle, like any real principle, is true regardless of personal circumstance or belief. That is why I feel that all of my previous letters might be helpful to any woman. But today I would like to show you that the feminine principle of woman as pleasure-giver is a corollary of a larger, cosmic principle: mankind was created by God for His pleasure, and the highest purpose of mankind is to give glory to God. Glory is given when we accurately reflect His nature and praise Him.

In our natural state we are totally unable to reflect God's nature except through the residual hints I mentioned before. For instance, almost all mothers love because they are created with that capacity, and in loving they reflect the loving nature of God who made love intrinsic to them. Or, our bodily beauty reflects God as artist, but indirectly. Furthermore, in our natural state we are most unlikely to praise God (complaining is more likely), or if we do praise Him, it is only ritualistically. God is a Spirit, and those who worship and praise Him must do so in their spirits and in truth. Our own spirit, that essential part that is usually categorized loosely with soul or mind, lies dormant or dead because of sin until it is awakened by God's Holy Spirit. This yearned-for awakening happens when Jesus is revealed to us as God's Son and the Christ, the Anointed One, who is sent to rescue the world from evil. More specifically, I become alive when my spirit is awakened to acknowledge that Jesus is the Prince sent to die for me personally as the consequence of my own evil, which I want to turn away from forever. With this acknowledgment and my commitment to Him, God sends His Holy Spirit *into* me to dwell in my spirit and to begin the beautiful creative work of forming His nature within me. This is the only way that any creature since Adam finds his fulfillment. All else is frustration. Even the language knows it—that elusive "fulfillment" we all seek is the filling full with the joyous Spirit of God. When we are filled with His Spirit, we literally become new creatures, and the expression of His life within us becomes a reflection of His glory.

Praise is the language of the new life within. Praise is not a mental manufacture; it just bubbles up spontaneously like an internal, eternal spring. Anything else that ever appealed to me is forgotten as nothing when I am filled with the incomparable Holy Spirit of God. The allurements of the intellectual life become a noisy striving after wind; in its broadest sense, all intellectual endeavor is looking for that which is realized in Jesus. The material world recedes to its proper realm of objectivity—no longer need I invest any of my personhood in desiring a *thing*. Neither the emotions nor the rational process masters me anymore; my awakened spirit masters and uses them, as the original order of God intended.

In my new state it is my greatest pleasure to please God, and it is His desire that I please other creatures, beginning with my husband. I discover with delight that God has equipped me for pleasing in unique ways, and that many of my capacities for pleasing are clustered in the traits that we call feminine—hence, the feminine pleasure principle.

Men, too, of course, are created to image and praise God for His glory, but their capacities fall more largely within the power and authority realms. Together the masculine and feminine halves, committed to God and imaging His Son through the work of the Holy Spirit within them, will reflect a microcosmic picture of God to their children and to the society around them.

Let me differentiate here between characteristics and character. The Lord desires that each of us, male and female, be shaped after the likeness of His Son in our character; that is, that we become loving, peaceful, joyful, patient, forgiving, humble, obedient, and so on. But characteristics are those propensities of ours to respond in individual ways, and they tend to be masculine or feminine. For instance, it is the will of God that both my husband and myself be humble-minded like Jesus. One of my husband's modes of expressing that humility might be good humor in the face of criticism from his confreres; one of my modes might be the restraint of my surging opinions in a conversational group. Each of us is allowing God's humility (character) to work out through traits of our personalities (characteristics). My feminine characteristics were yearning with the rest of creation for the revelation of God's Spirit within, so that they might find their true intent and expression, *i.e.*, glorification of their Maker.

The indwelling Spirit of God brings liberation— from evil, from habit, from suppression, oppression, depression, from self, from all. The Liberator is Jesus, who is total victory. The common error of all those frustrated persons who band together or lobby for power against whatever they see as the enemy is that they do not realize that united impotence is still impotent. One form of slavery may be exchanged for another, but it remains slavery. The feminist is not seeking freedom from the oppression of a sexist society only; that is one of the agents oppressing her. She needs total liberation and fulfillment. Then she is free to sing for joy while the walls of circumstance tumble down around her. This release to life can be yours, mine, anyone's. God does not run a merit system. His gifts are by grace. I will write soon to tell you how His grace has begun to work through my feminine nature.

Gratefully,
Judith

Dear Judith

A miracle has happened. I asked Jesus to forgive my sins and to be the Master of me, and immediately I knew that He had heard and that my spirit had become eternally alive. I feel as though I had never been alive at all before. I guess I don't have to explain to you the wonder of what happened. I tried to tell Peter, but he just said, "That's great, if that's what turns you on, Baby." He really didn't understand the cosmic importance of it. God in me—I can't comprehend it, but I know it is true.

The very next day a new girl was transferred into our department, and I knew instantly that she was a Christian too! Isn't that spooky? So we've been talking together and she's introduced me to some of her friends. Actually, Christians seem to be showing up everywhere, now that I'm looking. I didn't know that there were so many of us. I've been meeting with June (the new girl) and her friends to study the Bible and pray at noon.

But what shall I do about Peter? I find that I love him so much more now, and yet it is so painful to know that his spirit isn't alive. It's like you said before—I didn't know what I was seeking until I found Him, and Peter doesn't know either. I have a problem about Peter. I don't know how to say it so I'll just out with it. I've been feeling that he's still somehow unclean and this is affecting our sex life. How does a Christian deal with this? Please rush your reply.

In newness,
Anne

Dear Anne

I am praising and thanking God for your new life. It is the ultimate experience and yet only the beginning.

Another Peter has given us the answer to your first dilemma, and really to your second too. "Likewise you wives, be submissive to your husbands, so that some, though they do not obey the word, may be won *without a word* by the behavior of their wives, when they see your reverent and chaste behavior" (1 Pet. 3:1-2). I have emphasized "without a word" because that is where most wives go wrong in seeking to convert their husbands. Conversion is the work of the Holy Spirit. Pray for him constantly; thank God for him, and love him for all you are worth, including, and especially, physically. But don't preach to him or seek to teach him. That will only build resistance in his heart to the gospel, because he wants to be your leader and teacher, as God intended.

I am conscious as I write that what I understand about the nature of woman and marriage is only partial. I know this from experience because the revelation given to me grows each year as I live with a man and his children, but that which has been given to me over the past twenty years does not change; it is undergirded and built upon. A truth can be like a gemstone; we may carry the whole thing in our hand and yet never realize the intricate beauties within that wholly possessed entity. One of the still mysterious truths I hold is that in marriage the two become one. I "knew" this truth before I married, but how infinitely much more do I "know" this truth now! And much more "knowing" there must be yet to come.

The act of physical love is an unsurpassed expression of this oneness, but even sexual lovemaking is ancilliary to the real "oneness." Without the real oneness, sex would be laughable and ultimately depersonalizing. Now I do not mean that if the two are not in perfect harmony at all points, or if they do not feel their oneness, then sex is meaningless. Not at all. Their oneness is a fact despite their personal feelings. Sexual union may often stir up the realization of oneness when feelings are far afield plucking fantasy flowers. It is the notary stamp of a legal fact. Our tradition of common law recognizes this. It is, to borrow ecclesiastical terminology, "an outward sign of an inward grace." The real oneness I am speaking of is an inward grace.

We have all been educated to think in terms of orderly progressions toward goals. If one does steps one, two, and three in proper sequence, then one's goal should be achieved. This thinking has its limited usefulness in the material universe. However, God has a startling way of declaring accomplished facts about us before we can see them worked out in our experience. He is not limited by our conceptions of time and sequence. One of these startling facts is that we who have the new life of Christ in us are dead to sin; our experience tags along behind wide-eyed, runny-nosed, and reluctant. Another of those startling facts—a fiat from God—is that in marriage the two become one. Our experience of that fact follows along behind, either whining reluctantly or skipping along happily.

The oneness of a married couple is not a oneness like that of a chemical solution in which the two components lose their individual identities to become a third something else, such as the combination of salt and water which becomes as insipid saline solution. Married oneness is more like a lovely igneous rock, a welded whole in which the component minerals maintain their separate identities but greatly enhance one another. In the creation of the rock, it is evident that one mineral yielded to the coming of the other and conformed around it. Thus with woman and man. His personality is the thrusting, dominant one; hers is the receiving, yielding, caressing one. The wife in a rock or a marriage needs to be adaptable, flexible, and then the husband may incise an unknown and intricate vein as an extension of his creative powers, and the wise wife can relax and fully participate in his venture, knowing that the Creator has the whole process firmly in His hand. But as a creature with a will, the wife can harden herself against her husband's creative thrust and thwart his creative urges.

We see this truth acted out metaphorically in the sexual relationship. Thus, impotence and frigidity are symptoms of a wrongness in the inward relationship. They can be healed by the solidifying of the oneness. The oneness of a couple is actualized in experience by the cheerful cooperation and obedience of the wife in all of their multiple areas of relationship. This is her prerogative. She may negate, but not create, the oneness. In this she mirrors the negative capability of each created person to refuse the infusion of grace and life offered by his Creator; he cannot initiate life, but he can deny it. The stark symbolic drama of our choice between receiving or rejecting life is acted out repeatedly in every bedroom for us creatures of clay by our own selves. We rarely think of the sexual act as an earthly symbol for an altogether different spiritual process. This is the consistently powerfully attractive idea behind eroticism, which, of course, is a gross and evil distortion of God's intent. The sex act is a picture of our potential relationship to God, and we women are entrusted the role of the human person—yield for life or resist for eternal frustration. God gave us the sexual relationship for our pleasure, surely, but also for our teaching. How often in the Scriptures God uses the picture of himself as the Husband and the body of believers as the wife. The soul is a metaphoric she. The church is a metaphoric she. And she is only true as she is yielded and obedient.

The total poem of God as Lover of humanity is written. We are born, as women, with the capacity to become a living symbol in that eternal love poem, and thus to elucidate the poem for others. We may act our symbolic part with great joy or we may successfully lobby against production of *that* play in our neighborhood. In the latter case our audience may never know a symbol of anything but rebellion, stress, and striving, and the key to the poem is lost to them.

Oneness with God, reconciliation, is an accomplished

fact through the cross of Jesus Christ. Yet the appropriation of that oneness is forced on no one, and many scorn it. Oneness between husband and wife is also a fact that a marriage can be built on. The progressive revelation of oneness to the participants is a continual source of delight in both cases.

When I happily yield my body to my husband, I give him pleasure. When I willingly yield my opinions or desires to his, I give him a pleasure of a different sort. Both of these yieldings are a rich source of pleasure for me too. When a soul yields to the mastery of Jesus, God has pleasure, and the soul has pleasure. Jesus yielded himself to the will of the Father and pleased Him in all things. Yieldingness is essential to the giving of pleasure. That is why yieldingness is an essential part of the transcendent feminine principle.

> Lost and found in the delight of yielding,
> Judith

Dear Judith

We're both home tonight, and Peter is refinishing an antique dresser we found. He says to tell you to keep on writing your letters—whatever it is you are saying! I haven't been sharing them, naturally. I have been seeing him differently. I want to be one with Peter. I am *one with him*. And yet, yielding to him in all areas scares me. I mean, he's a great guy, but he's a human being and imperfect, and he still doesn't know the Lord's power. Another thing I'm scared of is becoming a blob—a meek, wishy-washy nothing. I can see that in some areas if my personality becomes softer, Peter will become stronger and more dynamic. For instance, when Bill and Penny were here I asked Peter for his opinion about a particular topic (abortion) before I jumped in with mine. I was amazed at what he said because I'd never known he thought that way about it.

I really cringed about the negative capability of women, because I can see that characteristic prominently in many women I know. It is their modus operandi. Whatever the situation, some women have an uncanny ability to see the negative side and then to sit on it. But I'd never made the connection between negative criticism and rebellion against God.

I want to be positive and yielded toward God. I want to be one with Peter. But I feel myself slipping into a chasm of passivity, and I'm clutching for my individuality. Can you help?

Love,
Anne

Dear Anne

Yieldingness is not passivity. A totally passive woman would be a bore to her mate, not a companion. We know that God cherishes us individually, that our uniqueness gives Him pleasure, and that we have been created fully equipped to give pleasure to our particular Adam. I have found that the limits set on my activity by my husband's wishes have all been beneficial. He is a protection to me from my own short-lived enthusiasms and poor judgment and from spiritual foes. Because of the duly instituted order in the universe, God will often make His will known to me through the wishes of my husband. This is one of the principles of good management; messages come down the hierarchy through the established order. How often I have obeyed my husband simply because of the principle of obedience only to find out later that I have escaped an entanglement or peril! This does not imply that my husband always has foreseen the consequences of my proposed action; the Lord may lead him to negate a plan for any number of reasons, some purely personal. As one's husband grows in spiritual perception, his guidance becomes more informed; but the Lord uses even the most ill-equipped husband to guide his submitted wife, simply because He stands behind His delegated authorities.

I remember as a working teen having been given the authority to order frozen foods for a very small store. In my inexperience I ordered two cases of frozen lima beans—nearly a lifetime supply for that slow market. Yet the manager did not chide me for my error. He upheld my decision just because he had given me an area of authority. God is like that with husbands. Only He is quite capable of causing a tremendous appetite for lima beans to arise in the neighborhood. He redeems the mistakes of His delegates. As wives we need only to obey and to trust the Redeemer.

The Eastern religions, and more recently the mind control and self-improvement seminars conducted in our own country, direct their adherents toward a state of passivity. This is not self-denial; it is self-abnegation. Self-denial implies the choice of a good greater than self. Passivity seeks nothingness. In direct contrast to passivity, the Holy Spirit brings a fullness to one's life, a completeness, a wholeness that prepares one to be actively creative in cooperation with the Source of all creativity. We know that beauty is defined by limits of shape and order; creative works happen within an ordered sphere. Thus a woman can only be truly creative when she is active within her prepared place, defined by her husband and her Creator. In the case of the single woman, or the widow, the corporate body—the church—is to fill this protective, authoritative, defining role for her.

The obedient wife lives in the optimal climate for

62

creativity, beauty, joy, faith, peace, and love to grow. Her bonds turn out to be garlands, her servitude a celebration. The world has a most curious idea that freedom is self-determination, even if the self is uninformed, untrustworthy, and blind, and the determination is an illusion playing into the hand of evil and leading ultimately to death. Chart the lives of the world's "free spirits" if you doubt this. The freedom that a wife has, living peacefully within the embrace of her husband's rule, is a type of the freedom the committed soul has within God's embrace. Indeed, the wife has the privileged position, a double freedom, the type and the real, the temporal and the eternal, the shadow and the substance. Consider these freedoms that accompany a love dependency: freedom from anxiety, worry, and fear; freedom from self-exaltation—a most wearisome endeavor; freedom from competition; freedom from the necessity to succeed; freedom from condemnation. When all those chains are dropped off, the soul can stretch in the sunshine and try her wings. As the male soul grows in his complete dependency on God, his freedom takes on its experiential reality too—we girls just have a helpful head start. Hopefully our joyful experience of freedom within rule will encourage a God-ward dependency in our male confreres.

The activities of the feminine soul within her sphere are infinite in variety, untouched by depressing enemies, untainted by the sordid. I know that each of us flits like an errant butterfly outside her hallowed sphere more or less frequently, but the dismal skies outside turn us back toward our own sunny fields. The woman who is freed within the restraint of love becomes so full of pleasure herself that her very nature becomes pleasure-giving. The sunny field is an internal state, and it "busts out all over." Her sense of humor is released; the happiest and funniest women that I know are those who are free in the care of their husbands and of God; they have the eternal perspective. Closely related is the constant welling up of thanksgiving and gratitude, first to God, secondly to husband. This spills over into praise, first to God, secondly to husband. Even as a bride I remember my wonderment that my husband had chosen me, had committed himself unreservedly to work in order to care for me, had made himself vulnerable for love's sake. I have never lost that sense of thankfulness to him, and to God for giving us to one another.

The happy and grateful woman is an optimistic one. She finds an unending supply of hope and cheerfulness, because her hope is ultimately in God himself, not her husband or other people. A woman secure under her husband's authority may actually be more adventuresome and innovative than her sister who imagines herself under no restraint. She can frolic in her sunny fields, a spendthrift of her talents and favors in loving and encouraging others, because she has no costly ego investments. More about my freedoms next time.

Actively,
Judith

Dear Judith

One of the freedoms that I've already experienced is freedom from condemnation. And the funny thing is that before I received Jesus as my Savior I never knew I was under condemnation! But I felt judged by everyone I met. Was I pretty enough? Was I smart enough? Was I dressed correctly? Did I say the right thing? I was putting off God's judgment of me on to them. Now that I know that I am forgiven of everything, I don't feel judged by people anymore, or rather, I don't care if they are judging me by people standards since I know that God is judging me by the Jesus standard!

I would like to be completely free from anxiety. One of our friends is a psychotherapist, and he thinks that anxiety is inevitable and is the motive behind production of any sort. But anxiety just seems to impede me when I'm out to accomplish anything.

I believe that I am grateful for Peter, such as he is, but I don't think I am grateful to him. He's very intelligent, very hard-working, witty, and warm. I don't see more of the image of God in him, except in embryo. Perhaps this is the most creative task I have before me right now, to allow that embryonic image to grow in freedom to its greatest clarity and fulfillment. My Adam, you say. Maybe the first direction I'd like to see him become is to be more adamant—more positive! But then, I guess, if he is God's workmanship, I'd better leave that to God. I certainly don't want to be plotting his reformation while I am learning to be submissive to God and to Peter—that would make me the condemner of my own lover, and, as you say, of my lord. That's hard to write! I'd like to write more, but I never seem to have enough time.

Gratefully,
Anne

Dear Anne

Another gift to the woman under authority is the gift of unhurried time. Popular bromides warn us that each man is created equal in the amount of time that he has to spend each day, presumably in doing constructive, successful activities. Nonsense. Time is infinitely expandable when it is given over to pleasure-giving. Our time, like our money, is eaten up by nonessentials without God's hand on us. When we are giving pleasure to Him and others, He explodes the minutes with a dazzling fission and lets us enter into an atomic time. How He does this is a mystery that calls me to worship and praise

66

Him even more. When you are overwhelmed with responsibilities and pressures, still yourself to praise Him. Just worship. Your moments will begin to grow, until you have time for everyone who has need of you, leisurely, graciously. I have to learn this principle over and over again myself when I slip back into busy frenzies.

I first discovered about expanding time as a young mother. We were attending a small mission church without a private place where I could nurse my tiny baby who was irritable and hungry—quite off schedule. There was a ten- or fifteen-minute break between Sunday school and the worship service. I decided to relax, take him home and feed him. This I did, with a conscious sense of trusting God for time. I drove home—at least five minutes—and back, and had a leisurely feeding and burping—usually a twenty minute process at minimum—and found that we were in church in plenty of time for the beginning hymn of the worship service. A small thing, yes, but I recall a real sense of having touched God's infinity.

There are, however, some very natural ways in which time is expanded for the pleasure-giver. The first is through her conscious choices. Whenever she chooses a pleasure-giving option, she is eliminating several nonprofitable, time-consuming options. When I choose, for instance, to sit through a Little League game, just so that my son will have someone on the bleachers who cares about him, I am eliminating the thorough perusal of the evening paper, which is seldom edifying anyway. A consistent set of pleasure-giving choices eliminates a whole spectrum of pleasure-seeking and time-consuming, if not pernicious, alternatives. I may regret that I never seem to have time for several attractive possibilities, perhaps a craft I would like to learn or a worthwhile civic organization or a bridge game with neighbors. But I can trust God to parcel out to me just enough pleasure-giving choices to fill out my times with His perfect will for me. My times are in His hand in perhaps a different way than for the besieged Psalmist.

This belief raises another most interesting question, however. I am convinced by my experience that God does indeed have a perfect plan for each moment of my life. I have the option of entering into His moment or refusing it. In fact, for a whole series of moments, hours—however long—I may be thinking, doing, acting quite apart from His plan for that segment of time. No matter if the activity I am doing seems good to me. At what point do I depart from God's perfect will and wander into His "permissive" will? If I spend the better part of a day in a frivolous activity, what was His perfect will for that wasted day? This whole question is resolved in the area of daily guidance, walking after the Spirit rather than after the flesh. It becomes progressively easier to know God's perfect will, and to delight in it. God help us in this respect!

Another quite natural way of expanding time is

through an altered perception of it. If one is caught in a traffic jam, for instance, the time is precious if it is perceived as a time for praying and praise. If I am delayed, and I am walking with the Spirit, I know that the delay is efficacious in some way, and so I can relax and enjoy the unexpected alteration in plans. Perhaps our greatest irritant is the invasions into our time by unwelcome elements. We see our time as fleeing away from us, quite out of our control, and we grasp at it greedily. This time-grabbing mentality is healed when eternity enters into our spirits. We, quite literally, have forever—forever to wait in line, forever to be polite to the telephone solicitor, forever to hear the neurotic complaint. It is precisely at this point that God's expansive miracle of time takes place. He always provides time to give away to the needy, enough and to spare. And God is infinitely patient and gracious; if we miss something the first time, He will send it around again. The perception of time is closely tied in with giving thanks in all circumstances. Anything that seems beyond our control is in God's benevolent control.

A further expansion of our time happens by multiple levels of usage. When I am content to do the perhaps unimaginative tasks which confront me as a woman—notably housework—I am free to use that same time for mental or spiritual activity. This is rarely possible for anyone encountering the pressures of competition and power-seeking. The ideal think-tank is a quiet home, with the husband at work, the children at school, and a schedule of routine, necessary physical activities to follow. Many of us allow the intrusions of radio and television to pierce our protective bubble of silence, however.

One other way I know of expanding time, halfway somewhere between the natural ways and God's supernatural interventions into the time particles. That is the way of redeeming time past. Anything that has occurred in the past is recorded in my memory and is accessible as a matter for prayer and thanksgiving. And Jesus, the Redeemer, is not limited by sequence and time. My prayer now about a remembered event can turn that event over to Him for a transformation into a positive good, if it was a sin or sadness, or into a trophy of praise, if it was a blessing even then. A past trauma is frequently turned by God into a rich source of compassion and understanding for a fellow who is suffering a like occurrence now. If we remember a past sin (God has forgotten them!), we can jubilate in God's forgiving grace demonstrated in that instance. A chance acquaintance hidden in the memory may keep popping up in one's consciousness—for intercessory prayer, of course! I wonder if a gracious God did not give us a memory to free us from chronology in our prayers. Our past hurts become immediately accessible to God's healing through prayer. Lay that one on your friend, the psychotherapist!

Timelessly,
Judith

Dear Judith

My moments haven't exploded yet—though some have fizzled—but I am beginning to see the possibilities in our busy life for a reevaluation of time. Peter and I are taking a weekend in the mountain country next week. I'm hoping that the scenery will strike him down to his knees with awe! Not really, but you know what I mean. I sometimes think he's getting more ornery as I try to be more yielding and loving to him. He wants to go fishing in the mountains. Eeeyuck!

I want to walk after the Spirit, but I usually don't know where He is going. How do I get to know His voice?

I've been thinking a lot about Jesus redeeming my past along the memory route. Not only did I thank Him for forgiving the sins I could remember, but I also found that I had a lot of forgiving to do as the memories came by. I have just been saying mentally, "I forgive X, Lord, for doing this or that to me. Please forgive X, too, and heal that hurt." I feel as though my guts are being washed out. It's great! Al, our psychotherapist friend, isn't ready for this yet. In fact, he thinks I've flipped out by becoming a Christian, but he's benignly superior.

Redeemed!
Anne

Dear Anne

Another mode of liberation available to the woman under authority is the freedom in quietness. This seems to be the very antithesis of most feminine natures. We are often talkative and very busy, and if we are not talking with our mouths and bodies, we are likely to be talking to ourselves on the inside. But God says that He values highly a woman's "meek and quiet spirit." And if He finds it precious, I want one.

The spirit, we know, is that innermost part of us that receives new life when God's Holy Spirit is breathed into us. So we know that the quietness is there, deep within, not in the outward circumstances. The children can be squabbling, the phone ringing, the dinner ruining, and yet in the spirit is a deep quiet. This is indeed supernatural. Quiet means rest, and my spirit is quiet when it rests in God. The wonderful secret to be shared is that one's spirit can rest in God *all* of the time, not only when the environment conforms to an ideal of peace and tranquility.

Even the most insensitive soul is occasionally quieted by the awesome stillness of nature—in a wood or lake or mountain. God's creation is endowed with the healing balm of natural beauty.

Poets always know this, and many try to approach God through the beauty-tranquility route. Though the natural creation does indeed attest to God's nature, it cannot reveal Him, as He is Spirit. In fact, the natural creation itself is waiting for us to be restored in spirit so that it may follow. Remember, nature was cursed when we fell. Man is the overseer. The trees and fields and rocks and waters, and the animal creation are peeping hopefully at you! The salutary effect of nature on a soul is a calming of his mind, emotions, and will from the outside in. This effect never reaches the spirit, because only spirit touches spirit. The true and lasting calming of the mind, emotions, and will comes from the resting spirit *outward* to them. Regenerated spirit was meant to lead the mind, emotion, will, and body, not to follow them. Only the Spirit of Jesus can please the Father. The reason He is pleased with a woman's quiet spirit is that by definition a quiet spirit is united with the Spirit of Jesus.

When my spirit is perfectly at rest in God, my mind, emotion, and will *must* follow, and my body follows them. No psychosomatic problems are possible in this perfect order. Thus the holy quietness begins to pervade my entire being. I think, I act, I feel, I decide, but from a core of cool stillness. I do not know what poise is until I am poised in God. Many times I slip back into allowing the control to pass from my spirit to the outer realm of mind, emotion, will, and body—and then chaos. This latter state is what Saint Paul calls walking after the flesh. I can only walk after the Spirit when I despair of myself and rely entirely on God's grace to do it in me.

Of course, each of us responds to her environment, and I am not disparaging the recreational effects of a walk or drive into the country, some garden work, a quiet home, sports participation, or restful music. These too are gifts of God for our refreshment. Perhaps when these calm our minds and emotion from the outside, we are prepared to listen to the insights of the quiet spirit within.

There are no "helps to a quiet spirit" that I know about. It comes as a grace from God—an outworking of the Holy Spirit within. Since God delights in a quiet spirit, we know that we can pray for one, and then begin to thank Him and praise Him for making provision for this and all things in the One Gift, His Son, Jesus. There are, however, four ways that I have discovered of placing myself in a position of yielded expectancy, that He might restore my spirit in that deep abiding place if He wills to do so. These ways are a process roughly parallel to making one's self beautiful in the boudoir. But then, the very desire to touch God is itself a boon and a grace from Him; sometimes I do not desire Him. Those four beauty secrets are the old "means of grace." Perhaps each soul must discover these on her own. Two are communal; two are private. The fellowship of other Christians for study, sharing, praise, and prayer is one; partaking of the Lord's Supper is another. The third is personal Bible reading, and the fourth is praying in the spirit. Each of these is an incalculable beautifier.

Listening is the desired outcome of quietness—that we might hear the internal voice of God when He chooses to speak within us. He speaks with a "still, small voice" that is easily lost in an internal state of din and dither. We are made able to commune directly with God's Holy Spirit when our own spirit is made alive by Him. Two names that we give to that internal communication are conscience and intuition. Conscience is laughingly referred to in the vernacular as the small voice within. I am repeatedly amazed when I discover some aspect of truth openly expressed in our common language and traditions, our cliches. All of our cliches must have been viable truths to the majority of society at some formative period. These truths are lifeless fossils to us, until each of us rediscovers them. The hearing of conscience is almost always more sensitively developed in women than in men. I believe that is because women are more apt to have a quiet spirit and, hence, *can* hear. The other mode of hearing God's voice is associated with yet another cliche—women's intuition. In God's plan there is no reason to suspect that men are not equally equipped for listening, if they will. It was Elijah who is recorded as hearing God in "a still, small voice." But we women are gifted with a special measure of intuition—when our spirits are quiet before God. A quiet spirit within us is not a luxury or an appurtenance; it is where the unsuspected, hidden rendezvous with God takes place, that we might receive and joyfully translate His directives into overflowing life. Each woman is a special courier, entrusted with life-and-death secrets. How sad if we miss the meeting because of our endless striving over trivia.

Quietly,
Judith

Dear Judith

I caught my first fish in the lake on this card. Fishing is a great tranquillizer. Peter was masterful with the boat, the tackle, the instructions, etc. I like the idea of quietness in my spirit, but meekness? You are precipitating an identity crisis again. Surely I am acceptable to God without forcing myself into the mold of meekness. That's not me—either in the old creation or the new. I have a cliche for you: "As the twig is bent, so grows the tree." And my bent is not meek!

Piscatorially (Peter's word),
Anne

Dear Anne

When a woman voluntarily places herself under the authority of God and her husband, she breaks the chain of compulsive hereditary and model patterning. "Like mother, like daughter" need no longer apply. She becomes uniquely new, as God intended her to be. We each have an inherent tendency to imitate a model. No education would ever take place if this were not true. We see this so clearly in pre-school children and chuckle warmheartedly. We are not amused when a mature woman is reenacting the unpleasant characteristics of her mother. After childhood, other models are substituted for the parent figure, but the imitator is stringently bound in the limits of his expression. Writers imitate models; artists reflect their masters; the world is made up of disciples in varying stages of development.

The only way to freedom from the severe limitations of our imitated masters is to imitate the Infinite One. His variety, goodness, beauty, justice, mercy, creativity are endless; hence, our imitation of Him is unique and original. No other imitation of Christ is growing exactly like mine, because no mortal can reflect more than a tiny fraction of the myriad, endless facets of the Divine Personality.

My originality must be found in Him, or else I have none. Without Him as my model and teacher, I am a melange of weak imitations of imperfect imitations. The rebellious soul who is sure that he is independent is in actuality imitating the defeated enemy, who also rebelled against God's glory. Ultimately, all of our models who are not themselves informed by the Spirit of Christ are imitators of the enemy. What a trap we mimics were into before God broke us out! Of course, God did not intend that we imitate His enemy, any more than we would wish our children to take after our opponent. But we have a clear choice, not *whether* to imitate or not, but *whom* to imitate. God rattles our boringly dismal chain of miserable imitations with the resounding principle of individual responsibility. We may choose our teacher. And if our parent-model does evil, we are able to switch our allegiance to righteousness. The contrary is true, too; the child of a righteous parent may choose to model himself after evil. And either may change again in his modeling, the righteous and the evil, in which case, the latter state counts.

Therefore it does not matter under grace whether one's mother were a domineering shrew or a humble pleaser to her husband. We still may choose our own course. The daughter of the submitted Christian mother will have the natural forces of imitation working for her as well as the supernatural that come into effect if she becomes an imitator of Christ. But God's Spirit is always sufficient; the daughter who was poorly patterned in her youth will have additional great cause for rejoicing as God's Spirit changes her. It is interesting that the modeling effect on the daughter of the righteous woman will tend to last, even if the daughter does not herself come under God's authority. She may well be a moral woman, if not a Christian. But she will tend toward the self-righteous, if she has not received Christ as her righteousness. This "halo" effect will have generally disappeared in the granddaughter unless she herself chooses to be renewed by God's Spirit. The granddaughter may, of course, imitate self-righteousness and moralism from her mother, and this can go on for generations. God's Spirit, however, is not passed on by the modeling process. Each generation must receive Him anew.

When a wife submits to her husband's authority, the influence of her parents and other models recedes into a proper perspective. The influence of a pernicious model, if one exists, is correspondingly diminished. In a submissive wife, those undesirable elements in her that might be an adverse model to her children will tend to be submerged or cancelled out, while the traits that make "good copy" will be enhanced.

As we women leave childhood, our proclivity for mimicking tends to embrace a broader "style of life"—one with which we would like to be identified, usually that of a social class just above our own. Society obliges by providing readily identifiable outward signs that we can appropriate to ourselves to flesh out our "image." We beg to participate in this imitative slavery, in clothing and hair fashions, in makeup, in home furnishings, in modes of transportation, in residences, in recreational pursuits, in entertaining—on and on. Our life becomes molded by the expectations, the criteria, that cluster around our adopted "life-style." Whether we are the motorcycle woman or the doctor's wife, we deny our freedom and submit to a tyranny of role expectations. The teen-age girl changes the object of her modeling behavior in a noticeable way from her mother to her peer group. But most of us are fixated there—we just change peer groups in an "upward" direction. Since we really want to be pleasing, the directives of a "life-style" relieve us from a lot of anxiety that comes from trying to get our cues in a cacaphony of stimuli all shouting, "Do it *this* way!" We make for ourselves a tenuous, shifting, unholy authority of the prevailing mode in our subculture. When we willingly place ourselves under the genuine authority of God and husband, we escape these other exacting gods.

When I am willingly under the authority of God and my husband, my desire is to please only them. I am truly liberated from many models and their demands. Others will be pleased with the spillover! God is pleased by the outworking of the Spirit of Jesus in my life. A pleasing life just happens by God's grace when I submit to Him. My husband surely will be pleased by the fruits of God's Spirit too. My behavior, then, in so far as I need *direct* my pleasing efforts, is formed by the requests and tastes of only one arbiter, my husband. The pressure is off. I soon become expert at pleasing him, or rather, it seems to please God that my husband be pleased with me, and He takes an active hand in arousing that pleasure. How easy it is to adapt to one man rather than bowing to many men and many fickle gods! God will use my husband as the frame, His Son as the model, His Spirit as the medium, and—voila!—I am an original.

Uniquely,
Judith

Dear Judith

Your theory of originality seems original to me, but I suspect that it is "merely" scriptural! I've been discovering lots of what you have to say in the Bible. That must be your written authority. What an amazing book! I find that each time I reread some verses that I've read before, God gives me some new understanding of the same words I understood differently, or rather, partially, before.

I've been looking hard at the choices I make and am disconcerted to discover that most of them are made for conforming reasons. But I don't want to look like a freak or live such a peculiar life-style that I will turn people away from Christianity. And then there's Peter. He likes a good-looking girl and a well-done house. I'm still fearful of losing him if I can't compete. Especially when he's gone—I get nervous and start imagining things. Peter is very attractive to other women too. If men are so responsive to pleasure-giving females, doesn't that leave him wide open to others who would love to please him for whatever personal need or gain they might have? Where does that leave me in all my meekness? The unfairness of this—of me being at the mercy of unscrupulous women just because I've given up my own unscrupulousness—infuriates me. I want to run from the whole arrangement and be alone again. I don't think of Peter as an automaton —he's "moral"—but the potential for breaking our union on his part is always there, and I feel frightened by it.

Honestly,
Anne

Dear Anne

Metaphor

One is *really* liberated when one becomes free from competitiveness and jealousy. These are two sides of the same gaudy mirror: one views from the magnifying side in pride, the other from the down-under side with covetousness. When we really see our uniqueness blossoming in the sunshine of God's authority, then we can appreciate the beauties and gifts of others without viewing them as a threat to ourselves and a diminution of our value. This is truly a work of grace when it begins to happen in your heart. A loving husband may accelerate the growth of this grace in a woman. She may feel securely rooted in his affection. But ultimately our security rests only with God, and when I know, really *know*, that I am His beloved, then I begin to rejoice with Him in His other beloveds and to love them.

For many years I was angry and rebellious over the instances of sanctioned polygamy in the Old Testament. David especially caused me pain in this respect because I loved him as a type of Christ. I believe that monogamy is clearly God's ideal state for marriage, but now I think that I see that God permitted polygamy in the Old Testament people in order to act out the spiritual truth of one God, many beloveds. If indeed sexual relationship is metaphoric, then we needed to view a Solomon with a thousand wives to apprehend the concept of God with His Bride, the Church, as a composite of many brides. Perhaps it is because of this symbolic identification of the husband with the Lord that adultery is always resident in the *woman*, who is symbolic of the created soul. Adultery symbolizes going after another god. It is the worshipping soul that makes the choice. The wife who is faithful to her own husband completes the picture of a soul faithful forever to the one God.

Apparently, in David's case, he was permitted to be "lord" to several wives, and as long as they were faithful to him, there was no adultery involved. The picture was one lord, many beloveds. But as soon as David broke into another man's symbolic acting out of the Lord and created soul relationship, the Uriah-Bathsheba union, then David took on the role of another god and spoiled the Uriah-Bathsheba symbol by adulterating her loyalty. Thus he sinned. It is evident where the double standard came from; it is the lustful distortion of a possibility inherent in the metaphoric nature of man and woman. How I would tremble, were I a male, at the very possibility of symbolically assuming the role of "other god"! The Lord hates adultery. The polygamy of the Old Testament is no longer necessary for typological or other reasons, because the perfect union of Christ and His composite bride is clearly understood. Jesus showed us that one husband with one wife is God's perfect plan for marriage.

Male jealousy aroused tends toward a violent possessiveness of his mate and a fierce anger at the interloper. This may hearken back to his metaphoric role, for God declares himself to be jealous over those who worship Him. However, man's jealousy is not pure; it is spoiled by sin. Female jealousy aroused, however, tends to be more fearful—afraid that someone or something might attract one's mate. Metaphorically and practically, it is unlovely and unnecessary. Just as I can trust God completely because of His nature,

I can trust my husband unreservedly. Whether or not he is worthy of trust is between him and God; it is not my concern or responsibility. My husband must account for his actions to God, but God is his head, not me. I am freed to relate to him openly, without suspicion, without questioning, without anxiety. Impossible? Yes, without the Holy Spirit. Very possible with Him. If a wholly trusted husband were to sin in adultery, I am sure the Christian wife would be deeply grieved, even as the Holy Spirit is grieved by sin. But I am sure that God would supply the grace of forgiveness, and the husband might be wholly trusted still.

As long as we see ourselves as competing for our husband's love, or for God's favor, or for the attention at a party, or for the approval of a group, we can never love the other "competitors." But when we become aware of the infinity of riches within us when we are filled with the incomparable Spirit of God, our own worldly configuration becomes a most insignificant thing. We are infinitely valued in Him. How could we ever be boring or empty—as long as He is in us? Cleopatra's "infinite variety" was miniscule compared to that which is in Him. We can relax and draw on His treasure. Let youth flee and all the vanities of worldly life with it. All yet remains when I see that my place in the sun is wholly within the Son. As I grow in knowledge of Him, whole new realms of light and life open to my consciousness. I begin to understand; I can discern that which remains hidden to the natural mind.

Competitive jealousy—the outworking of pride—
is the root sin. Satan competed with God for His
power and glory. Eve reiterated that sin for the
first of many repetitions. Not only was she tempted
by the serpent to compete with God in the matter
of knowledge, but she also was competing with
her husband for leadership when she acted without
consulting him. These temptations are relived by
every woman. First she has the option of submitting her mind to God's authority or of rejecting it.
Then she has the choice, if married, of striving
with her husband for the leadership role—which
she might easily win since he was born of a chain
of mothers that extends all the way back to Eve—
or of redeeming Eve's mistake. Submission to her
Adam will clear his vision, and he may stand at the
edge of a new garden where he can behold his own
potential as a renewed creature for becoming the
image of God. Christ in us is the new Adam. The
way of submission is the new Eve.

Yours for second chances,
Judith

Dear Judith

*I don't think I'll ever get over the feeling that Peter
somehow owes me marital faithfulness. But I will*

try to remember that he owes faithfulness, marital and otherwise, to God, not to me. In a way, that is more comfortable for me and less comfortable for Peter. He could, if he wished, outwit me and cheat very easily. God cannot be outwitted. But if I have no mandate to police him (that's the mother bit again), I can relax and turn his morals over to God and to Peter himself. Actually, I'd be most insulted if I thought Peter felt responsible for my moral behavior! Why hadn't I ever thought of it like this before? I've really been stupid and possessive in my fearfulness, not to mention presumptuous.

I thought at first as I read your thoughts about adultery being resident in the woman that that meant a man could have relations with an unmarried woman without violating God's metaphor. But, of course, that is not true, since many unmarried women are to be the wives of others, and a pre-marital encounter will spoil the later marriage union in one way or another. If a woman remains unmarried she still owes her total allegiance to God, if not to his "authorized representative." The principle remains the same.

Peter reads widely, as you know, and he's even picked up some books by modern churchmen. The sex ethic in them sounds very liberal and un-Christian to me. A meaningful commitment or a caring attitude seems to be the only qualification for sexual gratification to many who write in the name of Christianity. I can't square this with what the Bible says. It seems that much of the church is merely following the lead of the world in this area.

> *More freely than ever,*
> *Anne*

Dear Anne

I am grieved along with the Lord by the return in our sexual mores to paganism. Multiple relationships in the name of freedom, or sensitivity or heightened consciousness or openness or education or whatever, though increasingly promoted by many sociologists and psychologists, are named fornication and adultery by God, who always was somewhat of an Absolutist. Human nature is definitely limited in its imagination without the image of God himself to give light. The refinements of unenlightened intellect succumb, after all, to the old lusts of the flesh.

The defense for lifelong faithfulness to one spouse rests ultimately in the law of God. But we may know with confidence that His law is written into the very fibre of our bodies and into the fabric of our psychology. Because we are conformed to His laws by creation, departure from God's law leads to destruction, pain, loss, and disintegration. The life of the libertine ends in total disillusionment and despair. Death seems a release to him, but he is cruelly deluded by the evil one, for his pain and despair will be his for eternity.

Consider the argument of the strident woman, often in the context of a pro-abortion presentation, that her body is her own property. I tremble when I think of how utterly dependent we are on God's sustenance of physical life for each moment, each heartbeat, each breath. We did not create ourselves, nor any part of us. We are exclusively the property of our Creator and we live entirely at His pleasure. We are tenants "at will" in borrowed houses. To give another's property in an unsanctioned union is to invite God's wrath. Likewise, to cold-heartedly kill another embryonic body created within us—no matter how old—is the grossest kind of insensitivity to God's prerogatives. I *have* no rights to my own body. God is wholly justified in demanding perfect chastity. When He gives His permission to me to marry, He bestows certain rights to my body to my husband.

When a woman flaunts the protective proscriptions of God's plan of union only in marriage, her disintegration begins. She creates a discrepancy between her self-image and any ideal she has archetypically or historically from the Judeo-Christian ethic. She violates her conscience. Her abandonment of a moral ideal affects other traits of her personality structure, perhaps honesty, responsibility, unselfishness to begin with. The desecration of her body, which is meant to be the temple of her spirit and the Holy Spirit, causes her a shame that will lead her to harden her heart against hearing the truth of God. This in turn leads to intellectual befuddlement and all kinds of error. Permanent relationships that were intended by God to protect from loneliness and disillusionment are destroyed. Her future attractiveness is bound up with a rapidly aging body. Hope of eternity is destroyed. She devalues herself and becomes critical of others as a defense. Her natural inclination to be mastered by a strong husband and a benevolent Lord is continually frustrated. She becomes prey to many fears and has no protection. Her spirit is starved by an indulged body and an over-weening soul. And the experience of her multiple sexual unions never approaches the pleasure of an exclusive, totally committed relationship. For many women their serial encounters are simply boring. Then she begins to feel exploited and depersonalized and bitter toward lovers without commitment to her.

A marriage without exclusivity in sexual contacts is no real marriage. That must be why the Lord provided for divorce in the case of adultery—the marriage is already broken. If a woman has defiled her body, however, the Lord offers forgiveness freely if she wills to turn from sin to Him. And He, as the Redeemer, can restore her to purity. What grace there is for us in Jesus! The Lord calls men to purity too, of course.

In contrast to the bleakness of scattering one's sexual strength, the concentration and momentum of an on-going lifetime relationship is glorious. The mates in a faithful union preserve that which they have given of themselves in one another. The love which has strengthened him in the past is returned to strengthen her, and she returns his tenderness to him. They are vulnerable only to one another, but deeply vulnerable. Intimacy that is diluted loses its very essence, but intimacy protected intensifies continually. The security of a lifetime lover frees the energies of both husband and wife for creative and calm work with minds and bodies at rest in the sexual arena. This means in our culture that they ought to be at least fifty percent more effective than their prowling counterparts! Not the least benefit is freedom from guilt, which is vastly debilitating to many swingers. The children of faithful mates are spared unending confusion and pain and are given at least a running start toward a satisfying marriage of their own. But beyond all these secondary benefits, to be involved in a lasting love affair with one's own legal mate is most excruciatingly pleasurable, most delightfully economical and convenient, most free and good-humored, most sensitive and consciousness-raising, most blessed by the Lord, and that last, after all, is everything.

Where are all the proponents for the traditional, God-fearing "closed" marriage? Mostly they are at home, too content and happy to write noisome books. In the final analysis, Anne, even though my own protected path of marital fidelity is strewn with delights and the other way leads to destruction, my all-sufficient reason for marital fidelity is the same as Joseph's reason: how could I do this great sin against God, whom I love? I would far sooner deny passion forevermore than offend Him, the Beloved.

Faithfully,
Judith

Helping

Dear Judith

I know several friends who feel that the sex thing they are into is hopeless, and they really are despairing. What amazing grace that Jesus can restore us to purity, when we were sure we'd lost that forever. I just want to shout out to all those snared in adultery or homosexuality or whatever, "Hey! There's a way out! He's Jesus!" I think I'm becoming a fanatic.

From now on, it's got to be Peter and me exclusively, until death do us part. Oh, when will Peter see what we've really got? Maybe he does already in his quiet way. Peter has been rather tense lately. He has run into some difficulties at work. The man over him doesn't seem to appreciate Peter's best work. We think it is because he doesn't have enough expertise to understand what Peter is doing. So he has become obstructionistic. Peter is frustrated, naturally. We don't know if he can find another job in his specialty or if he should stay here and wait for his boss to be transferred somewhere, which is not too likely. I feel unable to help him in this and just sort of hold his hand over it all, especially since I don't want to preach at him. Peter could undercut his boss by showing him up as incompetent, but he is reluctant to do this, especially since the man has five children and a wife with cancer. Maybe God is getting Peter ready for something. Please help me to pray about this.

Love,
Anne

Dear Anne

The feminine principle of pleasure-giving is, paradoxically, also a protection to man, the protector. It seems to work like this: a woman who is quiet in her spirit and submissive to God and to her husband, waiting on their pleasure, gradually becomes a storehouse of wisdom and spiritual strength—which we all know is superior to physical strength. Day by day the Lord gives her new treasures to hide away. This is her business; she does not have to snatch moments where she can from other pursuits for a quick spiritual snack. Her supply is constantly growing and maturing as she daily feasts with the Lord. During times of stress she may well be able to provide from her surplus the spiritual stability, faith, hope, love, or optimistic outlook that is a deep resource to her husband, family, or friends. Not that she will suddenly emerge the real leader in a rapid *coup d'etat,* but within her center of quietness she knows the sustaining power of God's life, and circumstances cannot touch that life. She can communicate her certainty. She is like the munitions room within God's fortress. If she has been faithful in providing those about her with delights, if she is a real pleasure-giver, all the comforts and pleasures given hitherto were preparatory, really, to that time when she might provide something of God's treasure when it is sorely needed. She may serve bread a thousand times cheerfully so that when the moment comes she might break the Bread of Life for others. She may kiss and bandage a thousand small hurts so that when needed she might give the word of healing for a crucial, big hurt. Every winsome charm and grace is amply justified if the way is opened to a ministration of one of God's good gifts, and every courtesy is repaid if only one heart is softened toward Him. To be sweet and agreeable in the service of one's self-esteem is quite possible; to be sweet and agreeable as an appetizer for Him is a holy participation in God's eternal plan. The male who is busy buzzing about the beauty and fragrance of God's reflected personality in his mate will rarely desire the dark flowers of evil.

In a time of general moral decline, the influence of God and good is usually residual in at least some of the women. A return by women to solid virtue, a return to the Lord, will bring the men and children with them—by attraction, not coercion. I think that this is why countries, nations, and lands are "she's" in the languages. Those good qualities that make a strong character linger longest in us girls. Since the power of God is aligned with the right, men are protected, by God, for the sake of their righteous wives. God gives an entire nation a feminine posture. "She" either follows and pleases Him or leaves Him for other gods. The metaphor cuts both ways: a nation is like a woman because of her submissive (or rebellious) relationship to God, her Master; but then, godliness tends to become manifest first and last in the women of a nation because a woman is like the open land, receiving gladly the sunshine and rain of God's mercies. Of course, this tendency does not obviate the individual responsibility of the males one bit. I am just describing one phase of God's delivery system. The men who grow strong and lead God's people, including all the women, were often nurtured by a godly mother, grandmother, or teacher.

Thus it is so evident why feminine beauty must have the righteousness that comes from God. One of my favorite lines is "May she be as good as she is beautiful." Our persuasive potential as lovely women is prostituted if it is used for selfish or meaningless ends. Our beauty should become increasingly transparent, to open a window onto the altogether lovely One, who is purely beautiful. Our grace should be but an intimation of His grace. Our passion may hint at His consuming fire. And what we give of love, joy, and peace are but a few drops of sweet distillation from His great sea of love, joy, and peace.

The women's liberation movement is tending to draw the more articulate and energetic women into its vortex. That is because those who are more naturally talented are most susceptible to the sins of pride and independence. Since these women are the potential or actual mates of the more vigorous and talented men, the very heart of the power structure—the establishment, if you will—is under attack. Each woman who abdicates her position of moral suasion by herself becoming empty starves one or more males along with herself. As the "brain drain" (the "loss" of female talent to domesticity) is reversed, we are creating a multiplied moral drain that well may flush us all down the sewer. If the aggregate feminine beauty resource in our nation is expended on frivolity, materialism, and adulteries, rather than to delight toward righteousness, our impoverished country will not be able to stand. We ought to pray that the Lord of righteousness intervene directly. Again in the matter of intercessory prayer, it is most likely the quiet woman who takes the time and has the ear of God for her prayers. Indeed, the protection of the husband, the sons, the nation may be hidden in her prayer life. Quite possibly the destiny of our nation is decided over the kitchen sink in unseen prayer rather than in the President's cabinet. Remember always that the powers we see are a facade, and the real powers, Light and darkness, are spiritual. The no-account, downtrodden, submissive housewife of the libber's ridicule may be a real power-house with God, and she may be why God's mercy is yet extended to the accusing harridans.

Interestingly, a husband must be cognizant of and considerate of the deep spiritual grace within his own Christian wife or he may find his prayers hindered. I do not know why this is so, but it appears to be a protection for him. Perhaps if he is blind to the working of the Holy Spirit in the one nearest to him he is spiritually vulnerable and his prayers might be unwise. Finally, the ways of protection that a woman offers to a man, her protector, are most tenderly acted out during lovemaking, under the cover of submission.

Strong in my weakness,
Judith

Dear Judith

*Peter asked me to pray about his work problems!
I was most happy to oblige. I love that cautious,
stubborn fellow almost as much as God does. The
Lord was not slow in answering our prayers
(thanks for helping!). But His answer has thrown
me into a terrible dilemma. Peter has been offered
a position clear at the other end of the state. It is a
fine opportunity for him, as he would be the head
of the department and he would have freedom to
develop those creative ideas of his. I could see the
light of triumph in his eyes when he told me about
it. (He hasn't realized yet that God arranged the
offer.) Peter really wants to go, but he says we
won't go unless I sincerely want to. The burr in the
thing is that I've just been promoted at my work,
and our director talked with me for about twenty
minutes about how pleased they are with me. As
far as I can determine, no similar opportunity
exists for me there—in fact, my training and experience would be quite useless there. Though I
am a Christian, this panics me. Do you think God
requires this of me? How do I know that this offer
for Peter isn't a trick from the enemy to get me
away from what God wants me to do here at work?
I'd also have to leave my Christian friends and the*

only real people support I get, other than from you,
via mail. Keep on praying, please.

Wavering,
Anne

Dear Anne

Today I want to try out my "Joan the Baptist" theory on you. I am still testing it; perhaps you would like to examine some of the empirical evidences. Remember that in the Scriptures John the Baptist said that he must decrease so that Jesus would increase. This is also true in the believer's internal life; as the ego is diminished, the life of Jesus grows. But I theorize that this inverse relationship also exists in the natural between man and mate—as the wife decreases, the husband increases. Conversely, if the wife does not decrease, or if she increases herself, the husband is thwarted or diminished. In effect I am postulating a closed system composed of a man and a woman with a finite amount of energy. If the family energy is concentrated in the man's career, the family unit will rise and accelerate along whatever course it is taking. Inertia and drag are eliminated through the persistent helping of the unselfish wife.

In any living unit there are a number of time and energy-consuming tasks which must be done in order for life to be sustained at a reasonably comfortable level: the groceries must be procured and cooked; the clothing purchased and cleaned; the home furnished and kept up; the letters and bills written and mailed; the social and community contacts tended to; the automobiles and machines serviced, and so on. These activities are increased geometrically with the addition of each child. If these "basic living" tasks are divided equally between the partners, each partner is diminished in his career and creative potential. If the wife voluntarily assumes the major portion of the responsibility for the daily necessary chores, the husband is freed to develop his career choice fully, and the wife shares equally in the fruits. Furthermore, both wife and husband are also provided with a modest portion of discretionary time, and, if all is in order, they will be able to concentrate on their relationship with God and one another and their intensely imitative children.

In my observations, a two-career home tends to have two mediocre careers. There are exceptions, of course. But in those exceptions I wonder how the husband would have developed if he had had the full help of his mate. The early years together are the important ones. The picture changes when the man's career plans are established and the children are independent. I test this theory by observation: when I meet a young aggressive and successful career woman, I look to see what her husband is doing and if he has a haunted look about him. When I meet a very confident and successful man, I look for the woman behind him. That is a cliche, I know. But check it out for yourself. Those facts are the very ones that have the liberationists up in arms. But, Anne, the way of sacrifice for one another is God's way. And the way of self-denial is the secret path to all of the spiritual benefits of which I have been writing in my past letters. Then, also, it is much more pleasant to live with a lover than with a competitor.

As the husband is riding to his peak potential he requires, I believe, all of the available family energy supply. This is the launch, which in rockets as in husbands requires a great share of initial energy. After some years of sustained momentum, husbands tend to become stabilized in their chosen course. Their time of lessening energy demands tends to coincide with the time of increasing independence in the children. This is the time that a woman may wish to begin or resume a career of her own, if she can do so without jeopardizing the well-being of her husband or family. New factors influence the redistribution of family energy. One is the experience factor which releases increasing amounts of expendable energy over the years. The first chicken I cut and prepared for frying took an hour; the thousandth chicken is done with considerably less expenditure of time and energy. My husband's first public speech was a fairly large gobbler of his resources, and hence, family energy; now he speaks daily, extemporaneously, with little effort. Experience eases every area of life; that which was a minor crisis in our earlier years is handled routinely now.

Another releaser of new energy in the Christian family is the maturity factor. Neither he nor I consume the family energy supply on emotional binges. Neither is destructive of the other, but rather our energies are directed toward building up one another. Family energy is multiplied in this way, not diminished. A related factor is the increasing confidence factor. Worry or "contingency planning" consume minimal amounts of family energy. With a higher level of confidence, new experiences are incorporated easily.

The resource factor also increases as the years go by. Financial and material resources ease the burden on the family energy output. Long-standing friendships and professional acquaintances smooth away many obstacles. New opportunities seek out the family as a positive reputation builds. All of these factors, blessings from the Lord, accrue to the advantage of the wife as well as the advantage of the husband. They more than compensate the mature woman for her patient waiting, even though she begins her career fifteen or twenty years later than her impatient sister. One added irreplaceable asset is her quiet and gentle spirit, which could only have grown through her experience of humility and service.

If a wife does take on an outside job later in life,

she is under no pressure to succeed financially; she may choose to do what she likes best, as the Spirit leads her. A husband who has been faithfully upheld for many years will tend to be very supportive of his spouse's fledgling efforts and rather touchingly proud of her, not at all threatened as he might have been in his own unsure years. Her secure and relaxed personality and her personal maturity may advance her quickly in her later-life profession. Her relationship to her male co-workers and superiors will be chaste, sane, and friendly. Her wrought-in characteristic of willing service will make her a valued employee and friend, and she will find ample opportunities to help others. Hopefully, every vestige of nasty militancy will be gone from her personality and she is freed for cooperation.

Ponder these things with me, and if you are sure you were meant to have a career, perhaps you are right, but timing is crucial. Unbelievably good things come to

> She who waits,
> Judith

Dear Judith

Please forgive the delay in my writing. I hope we never have to move again! I don't know how we accumulated so much junk in three years. We've found a little house here that is just perfect for us. Most of our apartment things fit in fine, but I have lots more decorating and finding to do. Peter is very challenged and excited about his new work— "zesty" is the word I want.

The decision to come here has solved another problem that was between us. Peter wanted a family right away, but I wanted to wait. Now I can hardly wait. Why does it have to take three-quarters of a year? The house has three bedrooms—one for Peter's den and one for a nursery. The nursery is stuffed full of boxes right now.

So far I haven't had a moment's leisure time. I think I'm afraid of too much unscheduled time. Many of the things that I see housewives doing, especially older ones, seem wasteful and unappealing to me. I really don't want to become unproductive and trifling.

I haven't found any Christian fellowship here yet, as I don't want to go to a church without Peter. But I think maybe he's ready to suggest that we look around for a church. There are a couple of fellows at his work who are Christians. Isn't God great—and diplomatic?

> Love,
> Anne

Dear Anne

We women are usually relieved from the necessity of bread-winning and are given an array of options spread before us as a fruit basket of delicious fruits—ours to pick and choose, I mean for dessert—after we have taken care of the bread and butter preparations about the house and family. Our optional time grows from nearly none, when small children are ours, to the majority of our time, when the children are grown and the husband is firmly established in his career. When we find ourselves surprised with the gift of optional time after some years of adjustment to the responsibilities of homemaking and mothering, we may feel both pleasure and anxiety about the hours-beyond-necessity. What *should* we be doing with our "extra" energy, talent, training?

For many years our lives had been more or less ordered by necessity, often in a self-sacrificial way. Hopefully the selfish and vain girl that we were inside has been softened and shaped by God's hand through circumstance into someone who loves and gives as her very nature. There is a hint of this remodeling process for women in Saint Paul's cryptic remark to Timothy that a woman "will be saved through child-bearing, if she perseveres in faith and love and holiness, with modesty." We know that eternal life comes only through Christ Jesus, so this "saving" must be something else, more of a salvaging or restoration, perhaps for this life. The effect of rearing children is obvious in its salutary and maturing benefits for a woman's character—that is, if she takes her responsibility seriously. The process begins that first night at home with the new baby. When the late hour squawks begin, the young lady suddenly realizes this is *her* baby, and her personal comfort is secondary (even better, tertiary, if she is adapting well to her husband's needs). Since every decision for another at the expense of one's own comfort or desire is a degree toward the ideal of self-giving love, we mothers are trained almost in spite of ourselves. Never underestimate this homely school for character. It is one of those paradoxical blessings—in humiliation is exaltation. In this we imitate Christ.

But later, at the point of decision, when our "school master" says, in effect, that it is time for some electives, we may choose to continue our own rigorous training by finding others in need of our service, or we may begin to look in other departments. I see women taking up the following courses (there are surely others): Advanced Home and Self-Beautification with subheadings of crafts, sewing, fashion and cosmetics, decorating, gardening, and super-cleanliness; Academia Revisited, with themes of "I must have missed something back there"; Expanded Leisure, with classes in media entertainment, the arts, bridge, socializing, golf and other sports, clubbing (with or without a "noble" purpose) and reading; and Resumption of Interrupted Career. Many women dabble in all of these; some become specialists. It is at this point in life that the well-cared-for middle or upper-class woman is as free as any human being can be in the natural sense, as she is freed from the economic necessity of time-consuming labor. Not so, of course, for the poor or for most males.

God has promised His renewed children an abundant and free life. I feel that any of the leisure-time options are provided for our tasting, but they are not to devour us. If we hold them, we hold them lightly, ready to drop them if the Spirit should direct us. Instead of exploding with praise and gratitude to God and husband for this time of freedom, many women bind themselves with the chains of strange, competitive gods (any of these options may become an obsession) and are miserable and discontent. The problem, of course, is a spiritual one. Nothing satisfies the immortal but the Infinite. When the frantic pace of early wife-and-motherhood slows down, the unfulfilled woman has time to measure her vast emptiness. Perhaps she becomes so busy substituting her options for the earlier necessities that she postpones facing that endless abyss inside herself. Some take alcohol or drugs, some, a lover. Many launch out into a flurry of worthy causes and feel that they are far superior to the more frivolous pastimes of their sisters. But none of these optional activities satisfies, though they may dull the hunger for awhile.

The only activity or work that ultimately satisfies does not even sound like an activity or a work; it is to belive in Jesus. That's all. You see, all of the other options I have mentioned, and those I have forgotten, spring from the seeds of the flesh, and though they may pleasantly pass the time, they lead to, or end in, death. The seed of belief in Jesus proliferates into another kind of life. Some of the activities that proceed from belief may superficially resemble the activities of the flesh, but they are radically different. The difference is discernible only to one who is filled with the Holy Spirit because he too has believed in Jesus. The only work that God requires of us is to believe in the Son. Now we can relax, breathe deeply, and wait. Soon something small from God will appear on the horizon, something we may choose to do. It has the exhilarating life of the Spirit in it. That satisfying activity is followed by another God-sent option. I begin to look for them, eagerly, excitedly. The opportunities for life-filled activity continue to come, and, as I choose them, they satisfy deeply. Many of the options are openly worship; others are ministrations to man rather than directly toward God.

These Spirit-directed options are my rare, fragrant flowers scattered among the artificial flowers I see all around me. But I still pick the phony flowers sometimes and find them lifeless. How long until my choices are inerrantly for the real flowers? How often must I clutch the plastic red poppy when the real lily of the valley lies hidden close by? Why a too-constant phony daisy when a breathing rose is over the hillside? Alas! my eyes have plastic lenses and unless He gives them insight, they choose the gaudy rather than the godly. But, though we see partially now, we *do see.* And the scent of one real flower-option chosen will sustain us until the next. Perhaps we never will see our real choices on this earth clearly; the gentle intuition of the Holy Spirit in our spirit is so delicate, like a fleeting fragrance. I hope that I am sending along one or two real flowers for your own bouquet.

Lovingly,
Judith

Growing

Dear Judith

My remodeling process must have begun, because, thanks to our Lord, we are expecting a baby. Peter and I are both overwhelmed with the prospect—eager, yet filled with wondering. How do we know we will even be fit parents? Yet I know that our confidence can be in God. I still haven't seen much leisure time with all the fixing up to be done in our new home. Furthermore, I find that I'm incredibly sleepy and seem to need an afternoon nap. Already the baby has effected quite a life-change.

If the only work that satisfies is to believe in Jesus, then I'm in the satisfaction way. I do believe. I do! Perhaps that seed of belief is growing quietly now along with Peter's seed inside me. To be freed from the need of frenzied activity is a great freedom that I'd like to add to your list of freedoms for the liberated woman. God has sent me some opportunities to minister His life—mostly to Peter (indirectly), but also to my sister and to some others He has sent my way.

Actually, I'm rather relieved to have you say that you don't always know how to choose God's choices. I sometimes think that I'm not making any progress at all toward getting any better. Some of my same old sins keep hanging on.

We had an interesting experience last week when we went with Ron, a Christian who works with Peter, and his wife, Linda, to a Sunday evening fellowship meeting at a home. I knew at once that the group was really Christian because they seemed so joyful. There was a good Bible study with lots of input by everyone and some short prayers and some plain old friendship afterwards with coffee and cake. Peter seemed to enjoy the group. He likes Ron. Here's hoping, or praying, rather.

Expansively,
Anne

Dear Anne

Any true transformation of character, of our personhood, is a work done by the Holy Spirit in us as a consequence of our only work, believing in the Lord Jesus. Any other mode or promise of reformation is futile and illusory. Human maturation is a combination of at least two primary factors: experience in a natural sense, and experience of grace. Regrettably some close themselves to the latter and are stunted and grotesque in personality, even at an advanced age. It is meekly that I undertake to write what I know now of the Holy Spirit's working of character, as I am so conscious of being myself only a partially wrought creation. But perhaps the outworking of His grace in my life will be helpful to you, and my very partial observations may augment your own partial observations of His wonders.

The first and infallible sign of the Holy Spirit in

one's life is love, and because it is first in order and primacy, I will consider it last. Sufficient here is our mutual realization that nothing else happens without love, because God's very nature is love.

So let us first consider joy. Joy's source is the Lord and it makes us strong—strong because we sense its eternal nature and that nothing can overcome it. At its center it is jubilant and militant, though its expression may be very quiet indeed. Joy is the victory cry of Jesus in our inmost heart. Circumstances cannot touch joy, nor do they create or increase it. Joy is like a bomb bursting inside that breaks outward through walls of resisting flesh. It is accompanied by the absolute assurance that what God has said and done for us is, incredibly, completely true. Joy sings. It cannot do otherwise. What pitiable squeaks are any other sounds of music compared to the expressions of joy!

Though I had known deep soundings of joy before, how well I remember the morning when my imprisoned joy first burst out in singing. Everyone else was gone from the house except a bird belonging to one of the children and me. The bird almost burst for singing praises with me! Yes, the vocabulary of joy is praise. Praise to the Father, about His creation and goodness and care, and praise to Jesus for who He is and for His beautiful character and work for us. That joy has never left. It is always inside, ready to bubble up. Sometimes my emotions temporarily block it, but when I test it, it is always there. Joy is not emotional; happiness comes and goes, though one's happiness quotient surely increases when joy is released.

Christian groups are the only groups in which corporate joy is immediately apparent. Group joy draws the outsider like a sunny day. There is no real, lasting joy but that which comes with Jesus. That is why the angel announced to the shepherds, "Behold, I bring you tidings of great joy, for unto you is born this day a Savior, which is Christ, the Lord." Joy comes again to each individual with the new birth of Christ within him at the time of his conversion. That joy is released in expression when he is filled with the Holy Spirit.

Now it seems to me in my experience that the Holy Spirit imparts His climate in two ways: with sweeping largess, as a barometer might measure, and in gradations, as a thermometer might measure. Love is measured both barometrically and thermometrically. The character traits of the Spirit—patience, kindness, goodness, faithfulness, gentleness, and self-control—are formed in us by degrees and under pressure, as we abide in Christ. Our character is gradually transformed to be like the most lovely character of Jesus. These are thermometer fruits that ripen in time when the temperature rises.

But joy, and peace, are barometer gifts. If they are not in evidence, something is radically wrong. They are not gradual acquisitions over many arduous years of discipline and training. Joy and peace are just suddenly there—inside—as a pure act of merciful giving from God's own nature. They may be blocked by our own sin or willfulness, but they are not developed by degrees or experience. Surely our awareness of joy and peace can be deepened as we yield more completely to Him, but they are the end results of a completed fact, our redemption by the blood of Jesus Christ. Therefore they spring to life in us whole, fully formed. Joy is like an irrepressible Jack-in-the-box; the secret spring that moves it is the remembrance of what Jesus has already done for me. Joy and peace are barometer gifts in another way; they predict what is ahead of us. When we experience internal joy and peace suddenly given to us, whole and complete, without the slightest merit on our part, it dawns on us that Christ *is* our righteousness, and all of the other desired character traits *have* been given to us in Christ when we received Him. We need only to reckon ourselves dead to sin and alive with His life. This reckoning shoots up the thermometer, and quite unexpectedly we find ourselves being gentle, or patient, or kind, or good because the life of Jesus in us is that way.

Joy and peace are the high and low of our internal weather system. As in the natural barometric low, peace is revealed by stormy weather. The unshakeable peace of God "which passeth understanding" is the rock bottom that sustains all of our life experiences. Peace is the end of hostilities; it is the indissoluble agreement of amity between God and us written by the blood of Christ. With that ultimate peace declared and published, the skirmishes we face cannot touch us. How utterly irreplaceable is the peace that allows one to awake in the midst of a howling, crackling storm thinking, "Hello, Father. I love you. I am yours, no matter what. You are so great in majesty. Thank you, Father." Peace and joy accompany a double vision that the Spirit gives us. We begin to see spiritual reality as well as apparent circumstances. When we really "see" our victorious position in Christ, joy and peace are firmly established.

Our fullness of joy is contingent upon love for one another. Faith, grace, joy, and peace seem to be corporate gifts in the sense that they may be shared with other Christians without ever diminishing the supply. As a need develops in the body of Christ for faith or grace or joy or peace, other members can quickly provide. That is why fellowship is so crucial. That is why I am writing to you— to share God's joy and peace.

Openly,
Judith

Reaching

Dear Judith

I do know joy and peace, but intermittently. I must yet be blocking the power of God's Spirit in me somehow. Linda invited me to a ladies' daytime Bible fellowship, and I've gone twice. We are studying the book of Romans *there. I feel like chapter seven. I know that Christ is my righteousness, but my actions don't seem to have always gotten the message. I am very grateful to God for providing this new fellowship for me. There are about eight or nine girls who come.*

Peter is ridiculous. Even now he's shouting boy names at me as he's painting the nursery walls. They are all *boy names. Has it never occurred to him that some babies are born girls? Whatever will I do with him if God sends us a girl? What a chauvinist. He keeps putting his hands on my tummy to feel the kicking.*

I guess I've got the "barometer" fruits inside somewhere, but I can use a lot of help with the "thermometer" ones.

> *Love,*
> *Anne*

P.S. The nursery walls are blue, of course. Here's a smudge from Peter's brush.

Dear Anne   **Fruitfulness**

Now about those other fruits of the Holy Spirit, the ones that are revealed by degrees through heat and pressure—the thermometer fruits—patience, kindness, goodness, faithfulness, gentleness, and self-control. Trust the Holy Spirit to work these out in you through your experiences. His unique arranging of your environment. They are His fruit, not yours. If you pray for patience, watch for some very exasperating circumstance, probably a person. You see, the life of Christ in us is already patient beyond all comprehension, but we need to learn to reckon our flesh dead in that area and to let the life of Christ *be* our life, to truly abide in Him. The flesh does not like being dead and will contend for its forfeited rights. Never mind. Confess that Jesus in you is patient. Thank Him for His all-sufficient life, especially His patience. Praise Him for the circumstances that allow His patience to glorify Him. And His victorious life will triumph. You will know full well that you deserve no credit. Each added evidence of His life within you will increase your faith and joy. This is why we can thank the Lord for all circumstances and praise Him continually. Every trying time is ordered for His glory. We are not always aware of which fruit the Spirit is producing by a given circumstance. In His efficiency He may be growing several at once.

There seems to be a striking parallel between the Law, which we cannot of ourselves keep, and the fruit of the Holy Spirit in us, which is the positive expression of the Law. Joy and peace are the resultant fruit when we love God with all our heart and with all our soul and with all our mind—the first tablet of the Law. They indicate whether or not we are in a real love relationship with God. They measure the state of our entire system; that is why I call them barometer fruit. The other fruit correspond to the love of neighbor—the second tablet of the Law. Indeed, they can only be expressed in the company of others, hence they are experienced by degrees in our lives.

The vineyard of the Holy Spirit for the production of neighbor-fruit is centered in our homes—"where we live," as the vernacular would have it. For the pleasure-giving woman, willing submission to Christ and to the pruning of the Father are essential, that her home may be full of fruit. If she is a healthy, fruitful branch herself, she has the sap to transmit to the little branches, and an abundance of leaf, flower, and fruit to delight the husband with whom she is engrafted into the Vine. She becomes a co-worker with God in the home. Her gentleness, which is Christ's gentleness, fosters the growth of gentleness in those near her. Her forgiving patience, which is God's patience, props up a drooping tendril until it can drink of the Lord's refreshment. Her kindness, which is the outworking of Jesus' nature, may keep a wanderlust branch from straying from the Vine. Her faithfulness, which is God's gift, will hang on to the Vine securely in the violence of storm and be a stability to her neighboring branches. Her self-control, which is really Spirit-control, will give her a clear channel from the Stem to her dependents. Her goodness, which is Christ's righteousness, will attract the tender care of the Vinedresser to the branches near her, that they might be blessed. The branch does not have the source of supply in herself; she has, however, the fearful capacity to block off the flow of supply. The channel may become cluttered with trivia, or she may wound herself with sin. Without the life-sustaining flow from the Vine, no leaf or fruit will appear. She may resort to artifice to disguise the lack, but the Husbandman-Vinedresser and the husband will both know, and both will grieve, and the little vine tendrils will die.

When one catches the vision of how the Holy Spirit cultivates His fruit in us through the manipulation of our environment, the deep springs of a jolly good humor are undammed. The dire circumstance that would have caused us consternation before our initiation into His secret now causes us to applaud and appreciate His cleverness. We laugh with Him as He works our reformation. We may suspect, for instance, that we have a slight, insignificant problem with envy. Then He contrives for us to be literally thrown in with the epitome of all we have ever envied—our envy objectified and personified. This really superior person becomes so prominent in our thoughts that we are forced to face up with our sin, envy, and to confess it humbly before God, and to receive His healing. Without Ms. Superior, we would not have dealt with envious stirrings in us which were well known to God and displeasing to

Him. But how clever of God to have concocted just the right catalyst for our cleansing! And He has dealt with her in some significant way through the process. An insight into God's working with us creates a very humble good humor.

Perhaps we have allowed our "Irish temper" or "Italian temper" or "German temper" (or you fill in the ethnic designation for a thoroughly human temper) to have its outbursts. We have never allowed the resurrected Christ-nature in us to replace our temper, though it was included on the cross with Him. Surely God would allow the flesh this little endearing indulgence! Not so. He will arrange our environment so that our unleashed temper becomes so embarrassing to us as Christians and so obviously inconsistent with our confession that we face up to it, deal with it, and account it nailed with Christ. Then the patience and kindness of Jesus' life replaces that old "ethnic" hang-up.

All praise to the Beautiful Vine who makes His fruit through us!

Yours,
Judith, the pruned

Dear Judith

I have already met my Ms. Superior. She worked back in my office. Yes, God did use her to correct me, but not until you mentioned envy in your last letter. Now I've asked forgiveness for my envy, and each time I think of her I pray for her. I'm beginning to feel love for her during this process. Impossible!

I think that I envied her primarily because of her vast knowledge, not only in her own field but also her general knowledge. She also has a very easy way of expressing her knowledge—even though it is sometimes laced with sarcasm. Now I may be becoming covetous of another kind of knowledge— Bible knowledge. Some of the girls in our Wednesday morning group really know a lot about Christianity. They have read tons of books that I've never even heard about. There is one other girl besides Linda who seems to have a practical grasp of Christianity that I can't quite put my finger on. She and Linda also know Bible verses, but in a more complete, living sort of way. Can you relate to what I'm saying?

Peter and I have gone twice more to the Sunday evening fellowship with Ron and Linda. But the last time they met, Peter had to work on a paper at home. He's still in love with his job here. I'm glad for that.

Love in Jesus,
Anne

Dear Anne

My favorite intellectual (renewed variety) writes, "Knowledge puffs up, but love builds up." I think that we can see why the two are contrasted. The difference is like that between knowledge and wisdom. Whereas knowledge is accumulated information, wisdom and love are the practical outworkings of God's nature. I can understand all about a principle of the universe, but until I apply that knowledge in a creative way, my knowledge is an empty void. That empty knowledge, though, is capable of filling my mind, squandering my time, puffing my ego, and keeping me deeply involved in imaginary systems. It can, in short, effectively prevent me from adding so much as a brick to the work of God's kingdom.

Wisdom, in contrast, applies the knowledge of God's will to the task at hand, as the Spirit directs. Now—all libbers, please note—wisdom in the Scriptures is feminine, when she is personified.

122

What is it about wisdom that makes her feminine? She is meek and unselfish, not jealous or ambitious, and she is pure, peaceable, gentle, reasonable, certain, sincere, merciful, fruitful and righteous. These characteristics must add up to a "she" in God's mind. I praise Him for that potentiality. Would that each "she" were like her sister, Wisdom! Note how alike the characteristics of wisdom are to the characteristics of love—because each is Godlike and manifested perfectly in the person of Jesus. In practice, wisdom and love are inseparable. If I am moved to do the wise thing, it is also the loving thing. If I love truly, I love wisely. If I do wisely and lovingly, I give pleasure to God and others. But if I think correctly and do not act in love, I have knowledge, but no wisdom or love. Moreover, says Paul, if I have *all* knowledge but no love, I am nothing.

Perhaps God's teaching of the difference between knowledge and wisdom/love in my own life might make this crucial distinction clear. I am, in my natural self, inclined to accumulate knowledge, to sift it, to play with it, to glory in it. As a Christian, my natural propensity adjusted to my spirit's priorities and began to collect Bible knowledge. I was knowledgeable about the Lord's words concerning the care of orphans, the downtrodden, the sick, the weak, and so on. I was quite capable of speaking that Bible knowledge when I deemed it appropriate. Yet when I read a verse such as "Whoever receives this child in my name receives me . . ." I would be pierced in the heart, because I was knowledgeable without wisdom. Then I read, "Religion that is pure and undefiled before God and the Father is this: to visit orphans and widows in their affliction, and to keep oneself unstained from the world." Thought I, "Surely the Lord would not have given me academic kinds of capabilities if He meant for me to use my time ministering to little ones." I looked very hard, but could find no "except" clauses, such as, except if I have called you to glory in your knowledge, you are excused. Meanwhile, of course, I was praying for more love, as most Christians do. God was similarly dealing with my husband on this matter.

We would sometimes talk about how richly God had blessed us in our family life and agree that perhaps "someday" we ought to inquire into the possibility of having some foster children in our home. "Someday" would have to wait, of course, until I had accomplished certain academic goals. Ministering to the neighbor kids and teaching Sunday school and visiting the nursing home salved the conscience pricks. Nonetheless, God was interested in answering my prayers for wisdom and love, and He eventually gave me the grace to become obedient to His Word. We were accepted as a foster family and waited with much trepidation His first "little one." The Lord had just the right package of teen-age sinew and bone wrapped around quavering spirit and boisterous soul to accomplish that which He desired to do in us. Only through this often painful, often hilarious, always precarious, year-long experience did the Lord begin to flesh out my knowledge of those verses into wisdom and love. He continued the process with a succession of like encounters with Himself through serving others in our own home.

The wisdom and love inherent in those verses which I have thus experienced through ministering to His sent ones is still rudimentary, I know, compared to the vast riches of wisdom and love resident in Him. But it is tangibly real—an embodiment of knowledge. Never before, in many years of mind games, had knowledge for me been empowered to live, been transformed into action, as in this case. The process I am describing is possible because of the Word becoming Incarnate; because of Jesus, His words may become living and active in us. Myriad seeds are awaiting our comprehension in the Scriptures, waiting for the Living Water to explode them into life. Our obedience to the Word is the planting process in us.

The world values knowledge; it will even tolerate Bible knowledge without power. Ever since Eden, Eve has desired knowledge, and she is tempted to turn aside from her place as helpmeet to seek knowledge for herself. The temptation luring thousands of wives and mothers to desert or delegate their primary tasks in our time is a variation on the oldest devilish theme: why not seek out knowledge for yourself—surely God did not intend that you submit to this man's authority or stifle your own potential; surely you will not die if you seek self-actualization. The enemy is most subtle and crafty. The way of knowledge will increase self-esteem which becomes conceit which becomes pride, and pride separates us from God. But the way of love trains us to be self-less and humble minded. While we are building up others in the Kingdom of God, He comes to us and builds us up.

Only beginning to know love,
Judith

Sorrowing

Dear Judith

I'm writing from the hospital. I don't even know where to begin. The baby came too early and died. He was a boy. The Lord has been comforting me; I know it had to be His will for us. But Peter almost came apart. He tried so hard to support me, but he was crying himself (I'd never seen Peter cry), and he was almost speechless. I just wanted to comfort him, because I knew I was all right with Jesus to help me. After awhile Ron came and took Peter home with him. Then I knew that God had him in charge, and I could go to sleep.

Our Christian friends gave the Lord's own strength to us when we needed it. I have never felt so close to anyone other than Peter and my family. They have been coming to visit me here, two by two, and I love each of them so dearly. I've been lying here thinking about love and all the kinds there are. I love my Peter with every part of me. I've felt that our spirits were broken together by this sorrowful time.

Here comes the nurse.

Love,
Anne

Dear Anne

I am in sorrow with you about the baby. We can only know that God is perfect love, and He has acted from perfect love. I praise Him for sustaining you with His Comforter and by His servants. You have discovered some of God's love in your friends.

Each of us humans craves dear and true friends of both sexes. No bond of natural affiliation has ever approached the love created by the Holy Spirit between Christian brothers and sisters. How gnawingly incomplete become the contrived friendships of social or professional necessity or of accidental community of interest! That is because the Holy Spirit binds spirit to spirit in a Christian relationship, but even the most compatible of friends without Him have only a bond of soul to soul. The recognition of Himself in an instant that the Holy Spirit gives to my spirit when I meet another who has received Him is a joy-quickening phenomenon. It matters not in the least if a brother or sister is similar or dissimilar in background, tastes, personality, social status, education, sex, or appearance. The bond of the Spirit supersedes all of these claims or disclaimers to friendship.

God loves variety, and He enriches each member of His Body with friends who are, in a worldly view, very unlike himself. Perhaps I have never had much acquaintance with or interest in sheet-metal workers. But when I meet and love a brother who happens to work in sheet metal, I suddenly have compassion, interest, and good feelings for the whole class of sheet metal workers. In this way God expands our love for those still in the world. I remember being deeply touched by the embrace of a sister of another race—a stranger. We were near one another in a prayer meeting. As it closed, she turned to me in tears and hugged me. I knew intuitively that her gesture was one of love and forgiveness for the class or race I represented to her, and I thanked God for using me in that way, as a human symbol to work His grace in her. That particular sister I never saw again, as this occurred in another city; it was a momentary touching of the Spirit.

Those sisters and brothers with whom the Lord

allows us to live closely for an extended period of time become incredibly precious. We became as fond of their idiosyncrasies as we are of our own. Parting from them is most painful, yet the glorious hope of reunion in heaven makes it bearable. Even though one crosses the country or the world, the Lord has a ready-made family of brothers and sisters waiting. There is simply no metaphor adequate for the sweetness of Christian fellowship. And love for one another is a sure sign of the presence of the Holy Spirit in a group. Beware if there is no evidence of love between members of a church body.

A half-hour of praying and praising Jesus together and thanking the Father brings friends closer than a year of intellectual discussion. What deeper root of friendship could exist than the roots of a mutual Master, a mutual homeland, mutual siblings, a mutual philosophy, mutual goals, mutual experiences of grace and joy, a mutual guidebook, mutual problems, and above all, a mutual love for God and one another? Even if no word impresses an outsider, the love of Christians for one another will stir a longing in his heart. This love, agape love, is sufficient in itself to satisfy the deep need for love in every human being; it is the essence of love.

With some Christian brothers and sisters we discover that we have in addition a natural kind of friendship love for them. They may have the characteristics that are compatible with our characteristics on a mind-emotion-personality level, the soul level. Our friendship with them can be very pleasurable and helpful in our Christian life, especially in the sharing of problems. However, a natural affinity may sometimes lead the Christian friends into enjoying soulish communion with one another to the extent that they exclude other brothers and sisters, or neglect between themselves the frequent sharing of the richer treasures of the spirit. This is not likely to happen if the friends are totally immersed in the wonder of Jesus, though, because sharing about Him becomes much more interesting to them than any other topic of conversation.

When one has friendship strictly on a soul level (filial love) with those still of the world and one desires to share new discoveries of the spirit, the painful lack of real communication demonstrates "ears that do not hear" and exemplifies the notation of Paul that the Gospel is folly to them that are perishing but the very wisdom of God to those in Christ Jesus. When one is sorrowful over one natural friend who will not receive the Word of God, the Lord comforts us by sending ten friends who receive Him with gladness.

In a God-pleasing marriage the foundational love between Christian spirits is compounded by a filial love between souls and expressed physically in erotic love. Some worldly marriages survive, are even happy, with the bonding of souls and bodies. None are happy, that I know of, with merely an erotic bond. But a total fulfillment in marriage is realizable with the triple-bonding of spirit, soul, and body between Christian partners. I personally believe that a happy marriage is quite possible between Christians who have at first only the foundational love, the agape love. The commonality of interests of renewed persons and erotic love should follow. But marriage, after all, is lived in earthly bodies and with souls that are to be used in the service of God. It is a great blessing of God to have natural soul and body compatibilities in addition to spiritual love. Contrary to all outward evidences in our culture, the physical aspects are the *least* important. A dearly loved spirit and soul in one's mate should make any clean, God-created body quite attractive. Perhaps this is a feminine perspective, but if it were not so, our benevolent Lord would have created us all outwardly beautiful. The non-beautiful person is sure he is loved for his deeper qualities, but the very attractive one may be lured into some quite shallow relationships.

None of us can live without at least one kind of love. So much of the world is frantically looking for the least kind of love, the erotic, and eagerly hoping for the better kind of love, the filial or friendship love. The more perceptive worldlings know that the love of souls with or without erotic love is prerequisite for a lasting relationship. But the best, love between spirits, is reserved for God's renewed children, with or without the other loves. That is because our spirits are dead to Christian love until they are made alive by the coming of the Holy Spirit. The world has a vague and uninformed notion of spiritual union, acted out in such tragedies as suicide pacts. The less literate class uses spiritual terms for compliments and promises of enduring loyalty, especially in popular or country music. We can never thank God enough for making His multiple ways of love available to us.

Agape,
Judith

Dear Judith

Peter has a message for you: he says, "Jesus is Lord." Wait. He's corrected it. He says, "Tell her 'Jesus is my Lord!'" Oh, Judith! At last we are one in body, soul, and spirit! I cannot praise God enough for His mercy to us. This miracle happened when Peter was with Ron. I praise God for Ron and his faithfulness too. Peter is a new creature. That which I loved in him is beautifully enhanced and renewed, plus I see the new life of Jesus in him. God is so wonderfully wise to have allowed Ron to lead Peter into accepting Jesus as his Savior. Ron works with Peter every day and is a good personal friend. He's almost as happy as I am over Peter's new life.

Peter has accepted the death of the baby with more grace than I had imagined. Now we have begun to pray together for another child from the Lord. We both felt awkward about praying together out loud at first. We sort of sneaked into it by saying a thank you prayer before meals and gradually adding extemporaneous comments to the Lord while we were praying.

We've been going to the Sunday night fellowship and to Ron and Linda's church where the pastor and members are really alive Christians. Ron isn't the only evangelist there!

> *Still basking in God's love,*
> *Anne*

Dear Anne

Another aspect of love is nurturing love which on the natural level is expressed as parental love. Its spiritual parallel is the love of one who brings the word of God to someone for that person who receives the word. It is more than teacher for student affection; it is an engendering, creative, caring process. Sometimes circumstances are arranged so that the Christian who is used by the Holy Spirit to bring spiritual life to a lost one can remain nearby for months or years to watch over and aid the new baby's spiritual growth. At other times the Christian community as a whole receives that responsibility; the called evangelist brings spirits to life and then moves on. All members of the Body of Christ need one another to build up one another in the Lord, but the young members of the community are especially needy, because the stronger members will have learned how essential Bible reading, prayer, and fellowship are to their strength and will seek out these things themselves if they are deprived.

I want to be careful not to over-generalize here, Anne, but my observations have been that there is another correlation at work between the natural sexual role and the role of worker in the Kingdom of God. I believe that men are called to be evangelists, the sowers of seed, and women are called to be the nurturers of that sprouting seed. Of course, men nurture, too, just as in the parent role—with authority—but women by inclination and employments are seemingly more suited to the daily, on-going kind of love and attention (often very homely) that a new Christian thrives upon. Simply in terms of economy, men cannot usually drop their tasks at hand to minister again and again when the need arises. On the other hand, most women do more harm than good when they become aggressively evangelical. That is because men are hardly ever disposed to hear life-changing news from a woman, and women and children too are much more likely to respond to the Gospel given by a male, because he speaks with God's authority. Certainly there are times when the Spirit prompts a woman to give a quiet word of testimony about her Lord, and the Lord does use women to lead others to Jesus, especially other women and children. But I feel that a woman's usual role is as feeder and strengthener of those who are already begotten of the Spirit. It seems to work like this with us, at least. My husband is the more effective at leading new people to the Lord; he then turns them over to me, in a sense, for daily bread and butter sustenance, with him always available for the crises. There are those whom he must nurture by reason of his daily contacts, but I mean in our partnership efforts for the Lord. Likewise, God allows me ample opportunity to strengthen the faith of others separately from my husband.

I will risk postulating for you a "masculine style" evangelism and a "feminine style" evangelism. I am open to correction here (I hope everywhere!). The first confronts; the second attracts. The first administers the law if the sinner does not see his sin, and then directs him to God's forgiving grace. The second is so overflowing with love and joy that the sinner wants some too and asks where it is to be found. The first speaks with authority; the second woos with pleasant speech. In practice, both work together, but I feel that the natural gifts of men equip them best for "masculine style" evangelism and the natural tendencies of women make them better "feminine style" workers in the Lord's garden. Let the men be the bees, the women, the flowers.

Many Christian women feel under a heavy burden to accost every acquaintance or stranger with the Gospel. This burden makes them uncomfortable and awkward in casual social situations or even in the grocery store. Combined with a judgmental legalism, this attitude is poison to the world, and it accounts, I believe, for much of the world's conception of Christian fanaticism. Their forced contacts may be just enough to inoculate their prospects from a later, Holy Spirit directed encounter. We may be helping people to harden their hearts against the Holy Spirit. This is a most serious matter. It is so patently evident that nothing of the generative work of the Holy Spirit is ever done through soulish power. The Kingdom of Heaven is not taken by force of human will. If I am correct about the unseemliness of a woman confronting the world with God's Word when she is asked to win the world through love, then it is a double affront to God's dignity when a woman usurps a male prerogative and thrusts the Gospel without the bidding of the Holy Spirit.

A further consequence of women acting as aggressors in spiritual things is that the men will not step into their appointed functions as evangelists. But if women nurture faith and beam love and joy, they encourage the brothers to give heed to God's command to make disciples. Even in a basic husband and wife team, if, in a group situation, the wife is verbally the aggressor of the two, the husband will generally not enter fully into his role. A spiritually reticent man is often being held back by his own wife, though she privately is praying for him to "grow" in his Christian life. But if she were more femininely evangelical, her husband would be so thankful to God and so aware of his blessings that he would spontaneously begin to share the Gospel with others.

I am amazed that instructions on evangelism—all of the "methods" courses which are of limited usefulness, and then only at the behest of the Holy Spirit—ignore the sex difference of the potential evangelists. I think the result of such instruction is often frustration and anger for Christian women who are bidden to do their duty as Gospel-sharers in a masculine manner. The work of feeding and caring for God's children is just as crucial, but it seems to be despised and neglected in the Kingdom. The newly-born need daily spiritual food and lots of Christian love.

I pray that some of this that I write you will nurture your faith, as others have nurtured mine.

Almost parentally,
Judith

Dear Judith

Your letter has relieved me of a nagging feeling that I wasn't bold enough in my witnessing. When I first became a Christian I felt that I should speak to my boss about his sinful life and God's plan of salvation, but I was held back by, I thought, my own reticence. I do pray for him, though, and I'm trusting God to send the right witness to him just as he sent the right one for Peter. The Lord has given me several opportunities to speak up for Him. I'm helping Linda with a class of children, and I've been able to share at our Wednesday morning group and with my family. I've also fumbled a few times—I mean I've made some leading remarks about Jesus to unbelievers and have had them received very coldly. I have asked for His forgiveness if I've offended in His name. Perhaps the Lord's offensive team is in the males and His defensive team in the females!

Ron and Linda, who have been so helpful to us, have been telling us about the "fullness of the Holy Spirit" as an experience subsequent to salvation for them. They say, though, that the early church apparently experienced the fullness of the Holy Spirit at Pentecost and after that new converts got saved and filled at the same time. I'm con-

fused about this. Do you know what they are talking about? I know I already love God very much.

Love,
Anne

Dear Anne

That first and great commandment—to love the Lord with all one's heart and soul and mind—is the beginning and end of love. It is also impossible unless the Holy Spirit works that love of God within us. Our part is to make ourselves humble before Him. For many years as a Christian I loved the Lord as best I could. My friend the Holy Spirit was with me to help me to love Him, but my heart would wander from Him. Then I would grieve and He would grieve. At times I felt my heart would burst with love and appreciation for God, but at other times I would mingle with the world and get caught up in worldly pursuits—not especially sinful ones in themselves, but competitors to God for my love and attention. The chief competitor for the love of God in my heart was intellectualism. I would never consciously forsake loving the Lord; I would just get busy and interested in other things, and then I would discover one day that my love for Him had cooled a few degrees. I thank Him for the faithful ministry of His Word in those days, because time after time the embers of love would be fanned into flame by the preaching of His Word.

I have come to see, Anne, that when each of us Bible-believing Christians learns mentally or experiences spiritually something of God, he begins to assume that his perception of God is the correct and comprehensive one. He seeks out other Christians who have learned or experienced something of God in a way similar to his own communion with Him. Most of us are not humble before God; we will not confess that our idea of Him and our understanding of Scripture are partial and fallible. Though each of us realizes that other totally committed brothers and sisters see Him differently in some respects, we insist proudly that our perception is the true one. We may secretly suspect that either sin or stupidity has perverted our brother's appreciation of God. In this way we limit our relationship to Him, since we will not consider alternatives to our revelation. I do not mean that any revelation can be added to the Scriptures—which are complete and perfect—but we only understand them partially. God is far too great and unfathomable for any to understand or experience completely.

For many years as a Christian I assumed that my knowledge of God was neatly sufficient for life and doctrine. I cringe at the smugness of me! But God is merciful, and He moved, through our circumstances, to place my husband and me among Christians who knew Him in a fuller measure than we did. They gently showed us that we had not received all that Jesus had given to us, that we could have more of the Holy Spirit in our lives.

When I first heard that I was not experiencing the fullness of the Holy Spirit, I had two reactions. The first was a mistaken, defensive hurt for my Counselor, the Holy Spirit. How could anyone assume that He had not been with me hitherto, for I knew positively that He had? I knew that I could not believe without Him, but I also knew His unmistakable teaching of me through the Word, and I knew the sweetness of His presence in comfort, exhortation, guidance, and joy. My second reaction was a great openness toward Him—if indeed I could experience more of this wonderful Person, I wanted all of Him I could hold.

After diligently searching the Scriptures, my husband and I sought the filling of the Holy Spirit and submitted ourselves to a Spirit-filled brother for prayer. After we prayed simple prayers of request, based on Christ's righteousness, not our own, the brother laid his hands on our heads and Jesus filled us with His Holy Spirit in a new and powerful way.

That day was the beginning of a new walk with the Holy Spirit. He is the same Divine Counselor and Friend I knew and loved before, but now I know Him so much better. It is like the difference between courtship and marriage, between letter writing and personal visiting, between anticipating and participating, between a trickle of living water and streams of living water. His work of sanctification in me was no longer as hindered as before. It is possible to wash a dish with water teaspoonful by teaspoonful, but how much more efficient and satisfying it is to put the dish completely under a firm stream of water from the faucet. The most immediate evidence of His presence, however, was my greatly increased desire to praise God. Much of my inane thought life was instantly replaced by thoughts directed toward him. This was a very happy discovery! I began to see His hand in every aspect of my life. No longer did the prospect of heaven as a place for eternally praising God seem rather dull. An eternal life of praise had begun here on earth, and it was most pleasurable.

I include this from my own history with God to illustrate a hard-learned principle: God reveals himself when we humble ourselves before Him. When we assume that we have God figured out, we are far from Him. Perhaps this accounts for the sterility in many of our seminaries. The pattern of God's progressive revelation of Himself to me is not unique, but neither is it normative. As each Christian humbles himself before God and His Word, He will reveal Himself however He desires. This is not subjectivism. God remains unchangeable and the "objective reality," but He deals with us personally. Subjectivism interprets God according to the soul's little window on Him. Humility waits before God for God to expand one's perception of Him by breaking down the walls if necessary. Much of the time the Scriptures are the medium of the Holy Spirit's revelation; at all times the Scriptures are the standard and corrective for every spiritual experience.

Humility does not perceive God as an object and say to Him, "Thus far, and no further with me." Nor does humility boast of intimacy with God or flaunt His gifts, or reject the corrective influence of the larger Body of Christ, the church. If we love Him only with our mind, we reject His personality. If we love Him only with our heart, we may fall into doctrinal error. I know that God is far bigger than any of my faculties can begin to comprehend and that, as He gives me the grace to be humble before Him, He will increase my capacity to love Him with all my heart, soul, strength, and mind. I am so very grateful for what He has already graciously shown of Himself to me. I know He is lovingly willing to increase your love for Him, too.

Thankfully,
Judith

Dear Judith

I want to be as full of God's Holy Spirit as I can get and to love Him more and more. I know that my Christian life would be much easier to live with more of God's Spirit released in me. I really have to struggle to keep my faith at times, and to act like a Christian. The more I look into myself, the more discouraged I get. I keep remembering my background and reverting to my old daydreams. I can't figure out what's going on inside me.

Peter attended a men's prayer retreat with Ron, and while there he asked to be filled with the Holy Spirit. It seems as though he glows in the dark! I believe he has been spared months of trying hard to be a Christian. His calm assurance of the life of Jesus in him makes me want to experience more of the Lord.

Peter, dear beloved Peter, is the same quiet, rational person, but yet he's transformed.

In Christ's love,
Anne

Dear Anne

Introspection is a real enemy of loving God with the whole heart and soul and mind. Pursuing the pagan advice to "know thyself" is a fiat of psychology, education, and the arts and is diametrically opposed to the concentration of oneself to know God in His infinite richness and fullness. When one begins to know God, His light will teach us to know ourselves without our ever seeking self-knowledge. Our efforts to know are directed toward that which we love most. We are made for exclusivity in love; God says, for instance, that it is impossible to love both Him and money, since the kind of love He is speaking of is an all-consuming love. It is also impossible to love God as Master and to love self as master. We can, however, love self as a redeemed child of God and can love others as ourself because to do this is an extension of loving God.

If our thoughts are spent foolishly seeking to know ourselves, we get stuck in a morass of mental mud. The basic error of all psychotherapies is the attempt to create acceptance of, or reformation of, our old, sinful nature. Since our sinful nature is endlessly perverse, a lifetime cannot untangle the difficulties it has created and continues to create.

145

Only God can create a renewed life within us and make us new creatures in Christ.

When we are new creatures in Christ, however, the mind has its freedom to play where it will. The mind is no longer enslaved to sin; it can choose daily to be transformed by the power of the Living Christ within. We are urged by Saint Paul to think about whatever is true, honorable, just, pure, lovely, gracious, excellent, and praiseworthy. Those are godly things—they bear the lovable stamp of the nature of Jesus. To think about them is pure joy and often results in creative activity. As we grow in our love for God, our thought life becomes more and more delightful. However, at any point we retain the option of dwelling in our thought life back with the pigs. One of the happiests signs of the indwelling presence of the Holy Spirit to me was a radical change in the content of my dream life. All praise to God—I began to act like a Christian in my dreams!

Introspection seems a semi-respectable mode of operation to the unwary Christian. Surely we should be checking up on ourselves spiritually to see how we are doing! Wrong. We can ask God to show us where He wants a change to be made and He will search us and teach us without any further thought wasted on our part. Every moment that we are thinking about ourselves we are re-awakening the old self-nature from its death with Jesus, and we are excluding thoughts about and toward the Lord. I am convinced that the non-victorious

Christian is not the victim of excessive attack from the enemy, not the casualty of unbearably hard circumstances, but that he loses the battle in his thought life. Introspection is one of the most devastating blind alleys. I can say this with confidence since I am, in my natural self, an introspective person. I praise God that thinking about His infinite truths and beauties is becoming much more interesting than thinking about the real dullness of unregenerate life. It is true, however, that the inane is still mixed in with the sublime at this point in my walk with Him.

The focus of the renewed thought life is to be Jesus. We are being conformed to His image, which is the image of God. When we view Him with the steady adoring gaze of our thoughts, because we love Him, the wholly-to-be-desired process of change in us is effected by degrees. An image is only a true image when it is clear and undistorted. A real danger in introspection is that we are again gazing at a woefully imperfect model, the old self, and we may begin to revert in our imaging to that old, natural picture. We need to see Jesus constantly in our mind's eye in order to be becoming like Him. Jesus said if our eye be sound, our whole body will be full of light.

I have pondered how the Lord "scatters the proud in the imagination of their hearts." We know that the Lord says the imagination of the thoughts of man's heart is continually and only evil. If He allows us as natural men simply to dwell inwardly, then we are lost in only evil ruminations. The power of imagination to transform seems dependent on consistency and intensity. If God simply leaves us alone, our imagination is usually fragmented toward many evil diversions and models. We thwart the intent of God that we image forth His Son.

Some unregenerate men have the capacity to concentrate the evil imagination of their hearts to the extent of a coherent "vision" or system. These are the world's artists and geniuses. Yet their lives are ultimately meaningless because their visions are either distorted or accurate but evil, and therefore bound for destruction. The only alternative to imitating Christ is to imitate the evil one, whose chief characteristic is pride and rebellion.

As the renewed mind turns to contemplate the altogether lovely Jesus with increasing frequency, the universe begins to reveal its coherence around Him. He is the fixed point around which all else revolves. When we learn to focus on the Center of Reality our perspective is a true one. He is the Word for written or spoken expression. He is the Light for graphic expression. He is the Life in living matter. He is the Truth for scientific explanation. It is most interesting that the really basic questions in scientific inquiry remain unanswered, i.e., the association of word with meaning, the nature of light, the life-giving essence in living tissue, the power that causes atoms to integrate around a nucleus rather than to disintegrate. Each unsatisfied inquiry ultimately is satisfied by the person of Jesus active in the creation and sustaining of this physical world. Only the enlightened imagination fixed on Jesus can begin to apprehend this.

Finally, there is in my life a direct correlation of introspection with inactive depression and of fixating on Jesus with joyful expression. In my old Adamic nature is death; in Him is life and creation.

Looking at Him,
Judith

Dear Judith   **Waiting**

You are right. Looking mentally at Jesus is far more rewarding than looking at myself. I had not realized how ego-bound my mental habits had remained, even though I have the new life of Christ in me. I have set my heart and my mind to know Jesus only. I know that the fullness of God's Spirit will come when I am emptied of self. I also know that my despairing of self is also a work of God in me. I am thanking God for His provision of Jesus to be my fullness. I have yielded my whole self to Him, body, soul, and spirit. And now I am waiting in quietness for Him to come.

I feel a confidence leaping up in my heart that He has heard my prayer and that He is coming, bounding over the hills. When He comes in fullness to me, I know that I, too, will be able to sing of His grace from a full heart and that "my lips shall show forth his praise."

Peter is praying with me.

Waiting confidently,
Anne

Dear Anne

The feminine principle is, ultimately, the Christian principle. Each created soul must yield to the mastery of Jesus in order to receive life. There is no other way. Though the enemy, the serpent, has waged war against women from the beginning and has incited natural man to despise us, all men must become feminine in posture if they are to live, for the souls of men *and* women are comprehended in the Bride of Christ. As one dear brother said, "The men become brides of Christ and the women become sons of God." Ironically, though man is set on earth to mirror the power and authority of God, it is only through *submitting* to the infilling of the Holy Spirit that he receives real power. No man can please God without the Spirit of Jesus.

If the feminine principle is to give pleasure, and all creatures exist only to give pleasure to their Creator, then all males too, as creatures, continue to exist in a feminine dimension. It is to be expected that in an age of apostasy, females would downgrade submissive femininity and would seek a new definition of themselves without God. But there is no definition without God, either for female or male.

Each time a baby girl is born, a new incarnate picture of the human soul and of the human race is begun. She will visibly demonstrate the choices each soul, male or female, is permitted to make during a lifetime on this earth. She will grow either to become like the submitted and adorned Bride of Christ or like the harlot of Babylon. Without a beloved, incarnate model of submission and loyalty, the males of the world will not understand how to submit themselves to the mastery of God. Then both the women and the men will lose their identity which is only realizable in Him.

No woman or man is worthy to be the Bride of Christ, yet God himself takes the soul in her poverty, filth, and rags and prepares her himself to be His own. God's just anger against her sin is satisfied by His Son's own blood on the cross, so that He may deal with her according to His mercy. He washes her, perfumes her, and dresses her in white. He shares His name with her and takes her to be with Him forever in His home. He cares for her, protects her, loves her always. He communicates His very life to her. He gives her His credit card and trusts her to use it wisely. And she just desires to please Him. That's all. If she has an opportunity to do service for Him, she is overwhelmed with gratitude that she might in some small way show a measure of her love for Him. Now, Anne, how ever would we understand this potential relationship of soul with God for which we, male and female, were created if we never saw a godly and happy marriage? The metaphor of real life is the medium that the Holy Spirit uses to teach us the incomprehensible.

Why do you think the enemy attacks marriage so viciously? Do you think it matters a whit to him if we mortals spend our few moments on earth with or without a mate? No, he also knows that the living picture of an obedient, faithful wife and a loving husband will awaken an ineffable longing in human souls for union with Christ. And that desire becomes hope. And hope hears the Word with gladness and receives it. The Holy Spirit creates faith where the Word is heard. And faith in Christ and submission to Him brings us into union with Him. Praise God! Who are we that He should desire to love us so?

It is evident why the enemy must attack the human race through the women. Even though a male may be thoroughly corrupted from his potential to image God, a godly woman may still submit to him and mirror her part—the submission of a soul to God. The Lord will then intervene on her behalf.

We might have anticipated the new attempt to desecrate marriage in our time. In prior centuries women were abused and forced to submit; though this was outrageous behavior on the part of men, the final effect on women often was to turn their hearts in submission to God, and thus they were saved and through quiet submission and love showed others the joy of union with God. Now in these last times the attack is more subtle and is aimed at the center of God's metaphoric communication. The attack has moved from woman's circumstances inward to woman's submission. "Why should you not be your own authority?" asks the crafty enemy; "why not fulfill yourself?" If he succeeds in deceiving woman once again, he cuts off her longing for union with the ultimate authority, with Jesus, and hence, her life. She cannot then show any other soul, male or female, how to submit to Him.

Anne, my heart is anguished by the multitudes of our sisters who are being seduced away from their intended Bridegroom. As they seek independence and sexlessness, they are casting away that which is their most precious contribution to the symbolism of the universe: their ability to communicate to all humans in purity, humility, and softness the possibility of an eternal bridal life with God. Not to please God through the donning of Christ's wedding robes means death to herself. Not to please her husband may aid and abet death for him and their children. The Lord is coming for His spotless Bride; the feminine principle will be fully revealed at His coming. But before that time, be a friend to another Anne if you can see the vision of woman's irreplaceable role. Share the meaning of her unique womanhood with a sister who does not understand, that she too might yield to God and become one in His Bride. Teach her to love and obey her husband as never before, to keep her spirit in quietness, and to pray for others. Show her that love is active, and its first duty is to obey.

Woman is the beautiful paradox. She images the Christian paradox, the hidden Kingdom of God. For ". . . God chose what is weak in the world to shame the strong. God chose what is low and despised in the world, even things that are not, to bring to nothing things that are, so that no human being might boast in the presence of God. He is the source of your life in Christ Jesus, whom God made our wisdom, our righteousness and sanctification and redemption; therefore, as it is written, 'Let him who boasts, boast of the Lord.'"

                              In Jesus' Name,
                              Judith